CHILDCARE PROFESSIONALS

PRACTICAL CAREER GUIDES

Series Editor: Kezia Endsley

CHILDCARE PROFESSIONALS

A Practical Career Guide

TRACY BROWN HAMILTON

ROWMAN & LITTLEFIELD
Lanham • Boulder • New York • London

Published by Rowman & Littlefield
An imprint of The Rowman & Littlefield Publishing Group, Inc.
4501 Forbes Boulevard, Suite 200, Lanham, Maryland 20706
www.rowman.com

86-90 Paul Street, London EC2A 4NE, United Kingdom

British Library Cataloguing in Publication Information Available

Library of Congress Cataloging-in-Publication Data

Names: Hamilton, Tracy Brown, author.
Title: Childcare professionals : a practical career guide / Tracy Brown Hamilton.
Description: Lanham : Rowman & Littlefield, [2022] | Series: Practical career guides |
    Includes bibliographical references. | Summary: "Childcare Professionals: A Practical
    Career Guide covers the steps you need to take have a career in this field and includes
    interviews with professionals currently working in this field"—Provided by publisher.
Identifiers: LCCN 2021040416 (print) | LCCN 2021040417 (ebook) | ISBN
    9781538159262 (paperback) | ISBN 9781538159279 (epub)
Subjects: LCSH: Child care—Vocational guidance. | Child care workers.
Classification: LCC HQ778.5 .H36 2022 (print) | LCC HQ778.5 (ebook) | DDC
    362.7023—dc23/eng/20211108
LC record available at https://lccn.loc.gov/2021040416
LC ebook record available at https://lccn.loc.gov/2021040417

Contents

Introduction

So You Want a Career as a Childcare Professional

*I*f you enjoy spending time with children and helping them grow and develop, then a career as a childcare professional may be right for you. Caring for children can be a wonderfully rewarding job, and there are different career paths you can pursue to couple your ability and desire to work with children with other interests. For example, if you are really passionate about art, you can focus on teaching art to children. If you have a knack for business, you can think about starting your own day care service.

There is also room to grow in a childcare professional role, just as with any other field. In most jobs, people begin their careers in an entry-level role, such as becoming an assistant or completing a paid or unpaid internship or volunteer program, and slowly working their way up the ranks in the profession. Within the childcare realm, for example, maybe you are honing your natural skills with childcare as a babysitter, which could lead you to becoming a professional nanny or au pair or a preschool teacher. It could lead you to working for nonprofits or local organizations that work for the well-being of children.

That you have picked up this book and are reading it means you are considering a career as a childcare professional, which means you've already determined that working with children is something you might enjoy and feel you have an affinity for. That's already a great start to figuring out what you want from your future professional life.

Looking after children and working with them to learn and grow, looking after their physical needs, and helping them navigate their emotional and social development are not things just anyone can do. In fact, these are things a lot of people definitely cannot do—so you should already feel good that you have an interest in pursuing such an important role in society.

As well as being a satisfying and challenging career for reasons we will explore throughout the book, quality childcare professionals are very much in demand. Here are points to support how necessary qualified, dedicated child-care professionals are, and why the job is far more than "just" babysitting:

Childcare workers nurture, teach, and care for children who have not yet entered kindergarten. They also supervise older children before and after school. These workers play an important role in children's development by caring for them when their parents are at work or are away for other reasons or when the parents place their children in care to help them socialize with children their age.

In addition to attending to children's health, safety, and nutrition, childcare workers organize activities and implement curricula that stimulate children's physical, emotional, intellectual, and social growth. They help children explore individual interests, develop talents and independence, build self-esteem, learn how to get along with others, and prepare for more formal schooling.

- Childcare professionals nurture and teach children who have not yet entered kindergarten and therefore play a big part in preparing young children for entering formal school and succeeding there.
- Childcare professionals care for children from kindergarten upward before and after school if a parent or guardian is not able to because of job responsibilities or for any other reason, so they are often involved in providing assistance with homework or preparing children emotionally and otherwise to start their school day.
- Childcare professionals help children develop their social skills and emotional understanding and interaction with the world, taking the role of ensuring that a child is supported in these areas when the parent or guardian is not present.
- Childcare professionals guide children in exploring individual interests and strengths, developing talents and independence, and building self-esteem.

Being a childcare professional gives you the opportunity to help prepare children for school and life in a healthy, safe, supportive way. And for a parent or guardian, good childcare affords the ability to work and take care of personal needs with the assurance that the child is in good, trusting care.

This book is the ideal start for understanding the role of a childcare professional, the various environments in which they work, and what path you should follow to ensure you have all the training, education, and experience needed to succeed in your future career goals.

This book will help you understand how to begin now, whether you are a middle school or high school student or a university graduate, to set yourself on the course to a successful career as a childcare professional.

A Career as a Childcare Professional

You may think all careers that fall under the childcare professional label are the same, but that's never the case. Here are some of the career options available to you in the childcare professional field—all of which will be discussed in detail in this book:

- Day care provider
- Day care owner
- Nanny
- Preschool teacher
- Teaching assistant

Childcare professionals have various levels of training and certifications, depending on the type of work you want to do and where you want to work. This book will go into the options and requirements in more detail, but in general, a childcare professional is required to earn a high school diploma or equivalent, such as by passing the General Education Development (GED) test. To teach preschool, you will be expected to have earned at least a two-year college degree (called an associate degree) after high school.

Tip: Of course, to stand out from your colleagues and other aspiring childcare professionals, the more skills you bring—earning a first aid certification or speaking another language, such as Spanish or Arabic—the better. It's a good idea to be continuously learning, no matter what your career aspirations, so you leave all your options wide open.

The Market Today

How does the job market look for young people seeking to work as a childcare professional? According to the U.S. Bureau of Labor Statistics (BLS),[1] employment for childcare professionals is projected to grow 2 percent between 2019 and 2029. This is a lower rate of growth than average for an occupation—and a change from a previous BLS prediction that employment would grow 6.9 percent between 2016 and 2026. This could be in part due to the coronavirus pandemic, during which day care centers were forced to close and many parents worked from home. In any case, do not be discouraged by statistics. There will always be a demand for reliable and skilled childcare professionals.

Becoming a childcare professional brings with it a lot of satisfaction and responsibility as you take center stage in the emotional, physical, psychological, and other areas of developmental growth of children.
FatCamera/E +/Getty Images

What Does This Book Cover?

This book covers the following topics relating to childcare professional careers:

- Understanding what childcare professionals do and what characteristics many who work in this field possess
- How to form a career plan—starting now, wherever you are in your education—and how to start taking the steps that will best lead to success
- Educational and licensure requirements and opportunities and how to fulfill them
- Tips on writing your résumé, interviewing, networking, and applying for jobs
- Resources for further information

Where Do You Start?

As this book will show, no matter where you are in your education, from junior high to college graduate and beyond, it is never too soon to get started pursuing a career as a childcare professional. Whether you are spending time caring for children through babysitting in your community or volunteering to read to children at your local library, or learning about child development or earning a certification in first aid care, there are always steps you can take to prepare yourself for your future.

> "You have to be able to empathize and you have to be able to work together with others. Creativity and good physical health is also a must. In addition, it is very important that the atmosphere in the team is good. If the atmosphere is not good, you will immediately notice that from the behavior of the children." —Malou Kloet, childcare provider business owner and pedagogical coach

Once you've read this book, you will be well on your way to understanding what kind of career you want, what you can expect from it, and how to go about planning and beginning your path. Let's get started.

1

Why Choose a Career as a Childcare Professional?

*A*re you a patient person who does not always require things to go exactly to plan? Are you empathic and able to see and understand where someone else is coming from? Are you exceptionally reliable, able to take on a lot of responsibility, and confident and skilled enough to make important decisions? Are you interested in early child development? These are some key attributes that will help you succeed in and thoroughly enjoy a career as a childcare professional.

And here is probably the most important question when considering whether childcare as a career is for you: Do you have experience being around children and do you genuinely like being in their company?

If you are interested in learning more about childcare-related careers, this book is a great place to start. Choosing a career is a difficult task, but as will be discussed in more detail in chapter 2, there are many methods and means of support to help you refine your career goal and home in on a profession that will be satisfying and will fit you and your natural characteristics and interests the best.

Of course the first step is understanding what a particular field—in this case childcare—actually encompasses and informing yourself of how the future outlook of the profession looks. That is the emphasis of this chapter, which looks at defining the field in general and then more specific terms, as well as examining the past and predicted future of the field.

So as with any career, there are pros and cons, which will be discussed in the chapter. In balancing the good points and less attractive points of a career, you must ask yourself whether, in the end, the positive outweighs any negatives you may discover. This chapter will also help you decide whether a career in childcare is actually the right choice for you.

> **Note:** As with many careers but arguably more so, childcare professionals need to have a specific set of personal characteristics, because there is a lot at stake in the work they do: the safety of a child when their parent or guardian cannot be there to take care of them.

After reading this chapter, if you decide you are still interested in pursuing a career as a childcare professional, the next chapter will further offer suggestions for how to prepare your career path, including questions to ask yourself and resources to help you determine more specifically what kind of career within the childcare field suits you the very best.

What Are the Different Types of Childcare Professions Available?

As mentioned in the introduction, childcare professionals work in various environments. Childcare workers can work in their own homes, in the child's home, in childcare centers, or even in schools. They can work with infants, older children, children with specific development or physical challenges, or children who speak different languages. Some childcare workers move to other countries to look after children. There are many options available in the field, as well as many opportunities to grow in your career.

DAY CARE PROVIDER

In a nutshell, a day care provider is charged with caring for children before and after school hours or during the entire day if children are not yet attending school. Day care centers, where day care providers often work, provide this necessary service to working parents or guardians who are not available to look after their children during the hours they work. This care can also in some cases be provided in private homes that are licensed day care facilities. Therefore, the duties of a day care provider are broad: they help establish and enforce schedules or routines, assist with feeding and cleaning children, and encourage learning and socialization.

> **Note:** Working as a childcare provider doesn't necessarily mean working in a stand-alone business that provides childcare. Childcare as a service is provided more and more in places parents frequent, such as in some restaurants, hotels, gyms, and shopping malls.

DAY CARE OWNER

Very much related to day care providers, a day care owner is the person who actually owns and operates the business providing childcare. Day care owners may or may not also work directly with children, taking care of them exactly as a childcare provider does. But they are also responsible for running the business, managing relationships with parents, ensuring that bills and salaries are paid, recruiting and training staff, marketing the business, communicating with parents, ensuring that supplies such as diapers and nutritional foods are well stocked and on hand, and making sure the physical facilities are safe and well maintained.

> **Note:** There are laws about how many children a person can regularly provide child-care for in their home without obtaining official licensure to do so. In the state of Connecticut, for example, caring for even one child who is not a relative regularly for more than three hours a day requires a license to do so. Check carefully the rules in your state (or country if you live outside of the U.S.) before launching your childcare business in your home.

AU PAIR

Au pairs are a very specific type of childcare provider who have a very intimate relationship with the family they serve. Au pairs usually live with a family and are often from another country and working in exchange for room and board and to learn the native language of the country in which they work. An au pair does household chores as well as looking after children, including laundry, cleaning, and taking care of pets.

TIPS FOR BEING A GOOD BABYSITTER

Whether you have tons of experience either as an official babysitter or through look-ing after your own brothers or sisters, anyone who cares for children can use a healthy reminder of best practices for doing the job safely, responsibly, and comfort-ably—so that everyone can feel confident and enjoy the time on the job.

Here are eleven tips for being a good babysitter. The tips, provided by Healthline. com,[1] serve as a good overview for fulfilling your babysitter duties like a pro.

1. **Understand your comfort level**
   This is really important. Do not take a babysitting job just for the money. You have to be aware of and honest about your limitations. If there are expec-tations or needs the family has that you cannot meet—be they related to the age, number, or needs of the children or the hours you are being asked to work—be up front about this. Consider all factors before deciding if a family is a good fit for you and you for them.
2. **Communicate openly**
   You will not have points deducted for not knowing everything. In fact, cov-ering up when you are unsure or making decisions about things you don't feel you should is definitely the wrong thing to do when caring for other people's children. Always talk with the parents if you have any questions or face any issues. It can be simple things, like asking where you can find sunblock, or more complex issues, such as if you can't calm a highly upset child.
3. **Be prepared for anything**
   Safety is the number one responsibility of a babysitter. Be sure you know not only how to prevent and anticipate an emergency, but what to do in the case of one. Keep a list of phone numbers of contacts such as neighbors or family members. Know who to call in case of emergency, such as if you require medical help.
4. **Be informed**
   Keep yourself informed about possible dangers or situations you may not be anticipating. Talk with experienced babysitters or participate in a babysitting training course if there's one available in your area to get a deeper understanding of all the possibilities of situations that can arise when babysitting.

5. Be organized

This cannot be overstated! Kids thrive in environments that provide structure and routine. Of course they want to have fun and freedom within these parameters, but you do not want chaos and disorder. Keep to a regular schedule for naptimes, meals, outings. Know what the child or children should eat and should not. Have a clear agenda as much as possible.

6. Enjoy yourself and be active

Nobody wants the babysitter who sits playing on a phone the whole time or is otherwise not engaged with the children. A large part of your job is to play with or otherwise interact with the children. Perhaps doing crafts, going to a park, helping with homework—stay involved, stay active, and have fun. The hours will fly by more pleasantly for you as well.

7. Reinforce rules and limits

Similar to tip number 5, don't try too much to be the "fun babysitter"—stay in charge; be in control. Children may see your being there as an opportunity to "get away" with behaviors or activities that would not usually be allowed. They will try to push your limits. Be ready and be strong.

8. Be watchful

Keep your eye on the children you are taking care of as much as possible at all times. Accidents such as falls, burns, ingesting of poisons, and so on happen very quickly. Of course while multitasking, especially if you are looking after many children, it can be very difficult to do this, but always remember, the safety of the children is the priority over anything else that may serve as a distraction. Be able to prioritize where to put your focus.

9. Be open to criticism

In any job and in fact in any thing you do in your life, there will be people who observe you and will provide constructive criticism of your performance. Babysitting is no exception. Even if you do not think you are doing something "wrong," you may be doing something in a way other than the preference of your client (the child's parents). They are the boss. If they express criticism, take it and apply it, but do not get defensive or take it terribly personally.

10. Be gentle and caring

While a firm hand and maintaining your authority is important and actually fundamental to a babysitter's duties, that does not mean you cannot also be kind and warm. Children will respond better to you if you are not intimidating or do not seem angry or short tempered. Remember they are still learning and growing, and can be sensitive. Be upbeat, even if they make mistakes or disobey you.

11. **Be flexible**

Ah, flexible. That is another key characteristic of a successful, satisfied babysitter! While babysitting is rewarding, it can no doubt be challenging. Be able to go with the flow. Be prepared for emergencies, but also try and have a laid-back approach, at least outwardly, and don't expect things to go perfectly "to plan."

PRESCHOOL TEACHER

As the name implies, a preschool teacher is a person whose job it is to work with children in a classroom-like setting before they enter official school. The goal of preschool is to get young children ready for kindergarten through play, interactive activities with other children, and games. Language skills, vocabulary skills, social skills, and basic mathematical, scientific, and reading concepts are developed by having small-group lessons, or even one-on-one instruction.

Tip: Babysitting an infant, toddler, or child is a great way to gain experience in childcare and get a sense whether it is something you can envision yourself doing as a career. However, this "trial" needs to be safe for everyone involved. Before you task yourself with the full responsibility of another human life, see if you can spend time with the child and their parent together first, so you can learn firsthand what needs to be done, how to handle situations that may arise, and to develop a connection to the child and let the child equally get comfortable with you.

TEACHING ASSISTANT

Teaching assistants are not fully qualified teachers, but they do a lot of similar tasks. Teaching assistants provide support to teachers by helping to supervise children and activities in the classroom, and by working with children individually or in small groups. In some cases, teaching assistants work on a one-to-one basis with children with special educational needs that require additional focus.

Note: This book will not go into detail about teaching jobs beyond the preschool or assistant level. If you are interested in pursuing a career as a teacher, such as for elementary school–aged children, check out *Education Professionals: A Practical Career Guide* by Kezia Endsley, which covers the career path to that profession in more specific detail.

Childcare professionals serve individuals and communities by providing a safe, trusted environment for children while parents work, care for aging family members, or tend to other personal needs.
SolStock/iStock/Getty Images

CHILDCARE SERVICES IN THE U.S.: A BRIEF HISTORY

Like in many countries around the world, the question of who would care for children while their parents or parent were working became a very important one, particularly during the Industrial Revolution (starting around 1820) when more and more women were having to go to work to labor for long hours a day in factories. Prior to this period, women more commonly were staying at home to care for children during the day.

Once women were faced with either not working or leaving children at home alone, they had to rely on the charity of their communities for food and other necessities for survival, and this was not a long-term solution. It was during the latter part of the nineteenth century that actual day care began to be provided, also as a form of charity and means of offering some level of education—in some cases including religious education—to children.[2]

During the years of the Great Depression, the U.S. government organized national childcare facilities, providing relief work for teachers, custodians, cooks, nurses, and others who desperately needed employment. Unfortunately, these programs ended as soon as the Depression lifted.

Similar programs reemerged again during World War II, when many of the nation's women began working in the factories supporting the military stationed overseas. The Lanham Act of 1942–1946 was passed.[3] It was a law primarily for funding the war effort, but it included support for childcare centers in forty-one states. This was motivated by the fact that so many women had joined the workforce during the war, a time in which men who were previously working jobs at home had been shipped overseas to fight in the war. Women were an invaluable resource during this time (as today), but their working meant their children needed someone to watch them during the day.

These programs were also halted after the war ended, and women generally exited the workforce as the men returned home, and resumed their "traditional" role as homemakers and childcare givers. But of course this changed again, and today finding affordable childcare is a major issue for working parents in the U.S. Politicians such as Bernie Sanders have argued for nationally funded childcare in various forms, but to date, the Lanham Act represents the only time the U.S. had such a program to support working parents with funded childcare, as you see in other countries.

The Pros and Cons of Childcare Professional Careers

As with any career, one as a childcare professional carries with it upsides and downsides. But also true is that one person's "pro" is another person's "con." If you consider yourself a patient, reliable, curious, and positive person, childcare may be for you. If you feel excited about taking part in the development of children and playing a big role in how they learn, grow, and socialize—including ensuring that they eat well, are clean, are safe, and have their emotional needs respected and met—then you may be just the person the childcare profession needs.

If you enjoy a relaxed, quiet, and predictable environment in your workplace, and if you have a short fuse with sticky messes, loud noises, potential tantrums, and demanding clients, you may find that childcare is decidedly not for you. There are lots of aspects to consider when choosing the career that fits you well.

> **Tip:** Although it's one thing to read about the pros and cons of a particular career, the best way to really get a feel for what a typical day is like on the job and what the challenges and rewards are is to talk to someone who is already working in the profession, or who has in the past. This can also include spending time with someone who has a baby or young child, or who babysits.

Although there is a lot of variety within the childcare professional field (as far as who you care for, where, when, and using what methods), there are some generalizations that can be made when it comes to what is most challenging about the job and what is most gratifying.

Here are some general pros:

- If you enjoy children and are interested in child development, this is a career that will provide the opportunity to engage with children regularly and aid in and observe how they develop as young people during the period in which they are in your care.
- There will always be a need for childcare workers, so regardless of where you want to work (a school, a private business in your home, a day care center) you have a great shot at finding employment opportunities.

- You will have peers and colleagues who share your passion and from whom you can learn, as well as a job in which continually earning certifications and other qualifications is encouraged if not supported.
- It is a constantly evolving field with new trends and innovations and an endless opportunity for learning.
- You will be interacting with people on a very personal level, understanding the needs of their child or children and sharing in their care, and working with the demands of their schedules and preferences.

And here are some general cons:

- The working hours can be very early or very late in the day, and the days can be long.
- The work is intensive. It requires you to be on alert for potential crises while contributing to a calm, relaxed environment and remaining approachable and friendly to children and their parents.
- It is a high-pressure field that requires an ability to manage stress well as well as to multitask. It can also be emotionally draining, and you will need to protect yourself against burnout.
- The physical demands are high, as you will be expected to move around to play, to lead in activities. . . . Expect to stoop down, bend, kneel, and lift.

> "A typical day as a pedagogical teacher, business owner, and coach is that every day is different, chaotic, and beautiful at the same time. You never know what to expect, but wonderful moments always come." —Malou Kloet, childcare provider business owner and pedagogical coach

How Healthy Is the Job Market for Childcare Professionals?

The job market for childcare professionals is going through a bit of a strange patch, which may possibly be accounted for in part by the impacts of the

COVID-19 pandemic and the regulations and life changes—such as a steep, unprecedented rise in the number of people working at home and the closures of schools and childcare centers. Just a few years ago, statistics showed that the market for childcare professionals was expected to increase almost 7 percent between 2016 and 2026, which is as fast as average compared with other careers.[4]

However, more current data tells a different story. The Bureau of Labor Statistics[5] now predicts the childcare professional field to increase only 2 percent between 2019 and 2029, which is lower than average. This is with an average annual salary of $25,460 a year and $12.24 per hour. Although this news is not as good as earlier predictions, it is still an increase and circumstances can change. Do not let this number discourage you from a career calling—although of course salary and career outlook do play a part in the professional choices you make.

Working as a live-in nanny or au pair is an excellent opportunity to see a different part of the world, whether for the living-abroad chance alone or to study, while also gaining experience hands on in the childcare profession.
martin-dm/E +/Getty Images

Note: The average cost of child center–based childcare in the U.S. is $11,896 per year ($991 a month) for infants and $10,158 per year ($847 a month) for toddlers. Prices for infant day care can range from $5,760 to $20,880 a year ($480 to $1,740 monthly), according to ChildCare Aware of America.[6] So you can imagine what a significant decision a parent or parents face when deciding how to balance career with raising a family, in a practical, economic sense.

WHAT IS A MEDIAN INCOME?

Throughout your job search, you might hear the term "median income" used. What does it mean? Some people believe it's the same thing as "average income," but that's not correct. While the median income and average income might sometimes be similar, they are calculated in different ways.

The true definition of median income is the income at which half of the workers earn more than that income, and the other half of workers earn less. If this is complicated, think of it this way: Suppose there are five employees in a company, each with varying skills and experience. Here are their salaries:

- $42,500
- $48,250
- $51,600
- $63,120
- $86,325

What is the median income? In this case, the median income is $51,600, because of the five total positions listed, it is in the middle. Two salaries are higher than $51,600, and two are lower.

The "average income" is simply the total of all salaries, divided by the number of total jobs. In this case, the average income is $58,359.

Why does this matter? The median income is a more accurate way to measure the various incomes in a set because it's less likely to be influenced by extremely high or low numbers in the total group of salaries. For example, in our example of five incomes, the highest income ($86,325) is much higher than the other incomes, and therefore it makes the average income ($58,359) well higher than most incomes in the group. Therefore, if you base your income expectations on the average, you'll likely be disappointed to eventually learn that most incomes are below it.

But if you look at median income, you'll always know that half the people are above it, and half are below it. That way, depending on your level of experience and training, you'll have a better estimate of where you'll end up on the salary spectrum.

Am I Right for a Career as a Childcare Professional?

So, is a future as a childcare professional the right choice for you? This is a tough question to answer, because really the answer can only come from you. But don't despair: there are plenty of resources both online and elsewhere that can help you find the answer by guiding you through the types of questions and

Thinking about what kind of career suits you the best can feel frustrating and intimidating, because it requires you to ask yourself important questions that only you can answer. Carefully considering things like the type of people you want to surround yourself with and the environment in which you want to work can help you decide if a job is a good fit.
South_agency/E +/Getty Images

considerations that will help you understand the requirements of a particular job and what characteristics and commitments are required to succeed in it. Examples of these are covered in more detail in chapter 2.

For now, let's look at the general demands and responsibilities of a childcare career—as were mentioned previously in the section on pros and cons—and suggest some questions that may help you discover whether such a profession is a good match for your personality, your interests, and the general lifestyle you want to keep in the future.

Although there is not one "type" that matches the profile of a successful childcare professional, there are some aspects of the job that you can anticipate and think about whether it sounds like something you would naturally enjoy or expect to struggle with. It is particularly important, again, that you really consider these points, as it would be irresponsible and deeply unsatisfying to have a career in childcare if it is a forced fit for you.

> **Note:** Of course, no job is going to match your personality exactly or fit your every desire, especially when you are just starting out. There are, however, some aspects to a job that may be so unappealing or simply mismatched that you may decide to opt for something else, or equally you may be so drawn to a feature of a job that any downsides are not that important.

One way to see if you may be cut out for a career as a childcare professional is to ask yourself the following questions:

- *Do I genuinely like children?*
  This may seem obvious, but you simply cannot work with children if you do not feel a nature affinity for being with them and a deep interest in helping them develop. It is absolutely not the case that anybody can work with children, any more than anyone can perform brain surgery. Children do not always listen. They can loud, disruptive, angry, dirty, impolite, demanding, and aggressive. Children with developmental challenges can be require additional patience and understanding. If you work in childcare, there will be tantrums. There will diapers. There will be crying and stubbornness. If that sounds like an unmanageable night-mare to you, then you should rethink your choice.

- *Am I a gifted communicator who is approachable to both children and adults?*
  As a childcare professional, you will be doing a lot of communication: between you and a child or children, between you and the parents or grandparents, and, if you work in a day care center or other childcare business or learning center environment, you will be communicating with your manager and colleagues. You'll need to be able to effectively communicate information about the development, achievements, struggles, and growth of a child or children in professional terms, sometimes with parents who can be demanding or even combative.
- *Am I dependable and reliable?*
  Childcare professionals must be dependable and responsible. No parent will feel willing or comfortable trusting you with their pride and joy if you are not at minimum able to display that you can be trusted and counted on. It's absolutely imperative.

  If you don't feel you can be relied upon to take the responsibility of the safety and development of children, or are the right person to impact how they view themselves and the world, then you should reconsider your career choice.
- *At the same time, can I function under pressure?*
  Childcare is not the kind of profession that enables you to completely clear your schedule to focus on a specific task or predict how any particular day will go. When dealing directly with children, you have to be prepared for unpredictability in behavior, mood, health, energy, expectation, and so on. You are expected to keep your cool under pressure and to maintain your control over situations that arise.
- *Am I interested in pursuing additional training and earning qualifications throughout my career?*
  Training is a big part of childcare professions. If you work at a childcare facility, you will likely be expected to complete a childcare training that's specific to their needs or business promise. If you work for yourself and are committed to taking your career as far as possible, you should definitely plan to stay up to date with the latest training, trends, and certifications to really stand out and highlight your capabilities.

WEARING MANY HATS AS AN AWARD-WINNING NANNY

Candi Vajana.
Courtesy of Candi Vajana

Award-winning International Nanny of the Year 2017, newborn care specialist and nanny Candi Vajana has definitely traveled a varied career journey, and she has loved every minute of it. To anyone reading her CV, her career choices may seem a little disorganized or lacking in direction. It has always been clear to Candi, however, that she was building upon her experiences and from the lessons she learned traveling and living overseas, living and connecting with other cultures around the world. Candi is of the opinion that everyone has something to teach us.

Candi has worked as a nanny looking after children as young as newborns all the way to sixteen-year-olds; she has also worked in schools and in day cares.

How did you choose childcare as a career?

I always liked being around children, in particular babies and young children. When my parents had guests over, I would always hope for them to have young children. I also wanted to become a flight attendant, but that did not work out as I was too tall; when I was growing up there were different rules. So I decided that I should work with children. I was not sure in what capacity I wanted to work with children until my parents fostered a little girl who was two years old when she came to live with us. We did everything together. I was fifteen; we spent all our time together, and this experience made me realize that I wanted to work with children in a home setting rather than in a classroom. This little girl even came with me to look at schools and places to stay when it was time for me to attend college.

Can you describe your educational background and career path to date?

Once I made the decision to become a nanny, with my mother's help, I researched different schools that offered the [National Nursery Examination Board] NNEB training. Clearly Norland and Chiltern were the obvious choices as they are world-renowned schools. I did not want to ask my parents for financial help, so I chose to attend Eastbourne College of Arts and Technology in East Sussex, UK, and I think it was the best decision I ever made. The course was two years, and it covered everything related to children from before birth to age seven years. I learnt so much from the practicums we had; some were in classrooms, some were in homes, some were in maternity wards in hospitals. It was all very exciting and interesting.

Once I finished the course and I started working, I decided that I wanted to continue learning, so I enrolled in a TEFL course so that I could teach English as a foreign language, and once I completed that I went on to a Montessori teacher training course.

I continued to learn throughout my career; you can never know too much. I received an administrator credential to run a day care in the U.S., and I attended yearly classes in early childhood education.

I have a degree in business management, which I received from Anglia Ruskin University, and I am currently in my second year at the Open University for a degree in early childhood.

What is a typical day on the job for you?

My typical day is very busy. I am currently looking after one child who is in Key Stage 1 [five to seven years old] but is being homeschooled. It is an early wakeup to get ready before my charge [term for a child in one's care] wakes up; the family I work for travels extensively so we are always on the move and dealing with different time zones and new places. My charge and I spend the day together as my role is a rota role. This means I work for fourteen days twenty-four hours a day; I then switch with another nanny who does the same and we keep rotating.

The days can be long at times, especially if we are physically traveling, but we do enjoy each other's company so we giggle a lot and have fun. As a nanny, you have many responsibilities: you are responsible for the well-being of your charge, you are responsible for your charge's education, you are responsible for your charge's activities and building relationships with family members, which he or she may not see very often.

As a nanny, you wear many hats, and it is important to be able to do so.

What's the most challenging part or stressful part of your job?

The most challenging part of my job, I would say, is leaving the family. As time goes on, children grow, family dynamics change, and nannies do have to move on; this is the nature of the beast. Once you have formed an attachment to your charge and the family, it is extremely hard to say goodbye. It is like a period of mourning in a way, because you are saying goodbye to a part of your life and your heart.

What kinds of qualities and personal skills do you consider advantageous to doing your job successfully?

In order to be a successful nanny, there are many qualities and skills one should possess; really enjoying your job and loving what you do, I would say, is the most important one. I have seen so many nannies really not happy in their roles, and this trickles down to their charges. Being patient is another very important skill; children can test us, and being patient is definitely an ace up the sleeve. Being resourceful and caring; being trustworthy and respectful; being firm but fair, honest and up front, empathetic and calm.

Being able to set boundaries for the child, the family, and yourself is extremely important and a skill that comes with time. As a new nanny, when I first started working, I had no idea how to set boundaries for the parents.

How do you combat burnout?

This is the sixty-four-million-dollar question that we would all like to know the answer to! As a nanny, you end up taking on the world's problems because you are most likely an empathetic person, but this does not mean that you should not cut out time for yourself and make sure you are able to enjoy your life. There is a lot of talk in the nanny world about self-care and nanny burnout. I am not sure anyone has found the perfect solution; my suggestion is do what makes you happy, what keeps you sane, and what makes you relax!

═══════════════

Summary

This chapter covered a lot of ground as far as looking more closely as the various types of childcare professions and the roles and work environments available within the field. Here are some ideas to take away with you as you move on to the next chapter:

- One person's dream can be another's nightmare. It is absolutely a requirement for a career as a childcare professional that you genuinely love being around and working with children. If you can't imagine handling the responsibility, the messiness, the mood swings, the physical and emotional demands, you will not succeed in this. On the other hand, if the opposite is true, you will likely thrive in this profession and enjoy it fully.

- No two days are alike for a childcare professional, which makes it an exciting field in which you are continuously challenged and constantly learning.
- As a childcare professional, you can choose from different work environments, from schools to your home, from stand-alone day care centers to care providers in more specific locations like stores that provide child-minding services or gyms.
- Childcare professionals get to work with a variety of families from all backgrounds, age groups, socioeconomic and geographic circumstances, and career and educational levels.
- As a profession, childcare careers have a growth rate prediction of 2 percent between 2019 and 2029, which is not as strong as other careers. However, people will always be looking for quality, reliable childcare, so don't let this prediction put you off before you weigh it against all the pros and cons of this career choice.

Given all you now know about the job of a childcare professional, you may still be questioning whether such a career is right for you. This chapter provided some questions that can help you visualize yourself in real-world situations you can expect to face on the job, to help you guide your decision process.

Assuming you are now more enthusiastic than ever about pursuing a career as a childcare professional, in the next chapter we will look more closely at how you can refine your choice to a more specific job. It offers tips and advice and how to find the role and work environment that will be most satisfying to you, and what steps you can start taking—immediately!—toward reaching your future career goals.

2

Forming a Career Plan

Choosing a career may seem like one of the most difficult choices you will have to make, because it is one of the most important and there are so many options to consider. And it's exciting if you take the pressure off and just think of it as exploring the many options that you have in front of you.

Often, it's easy to narrow down what type of careers suit your interests and personality, as we've seen in chapter 1. Other times, you can imagine yourself in many seemingly different careers, which is why it's important to think about what kinds of skills or characteristics or interests are at the root of your career ambitions. And remember: not everyone chooses a career and then stays with it throughout one's working life. You may thrive happily in one profession throughout your career, or you may change along the way.

There are simply so many types of careers out there, and it is easy to feel overwhelmed. Particularly if you have many passions and interests, it can be hard to narrow your options down. If "working with children and making a difference" rank high on your list of qualities of a job that appeal to you, then childcare work is definitely worth looking into, and that you are reading this book means you have decided to investigate a career in the field more closely. Note also that childcare is the type of job that not everybody is suited for, and those who succeed the most in it are those who feel a genuine passion for it. So if you think that's you, it's definitely worth examining the possibilities.

Tip: Keep in mind as you consider your career options that it is common to change your mind or shift gears at any stage in your career. Be thoughtful about your decisions, but don't put too much pressure on yourself. It's not a case of only getting one chance to decide.

A career in childcare work is in some ways a very specific choice of career, but it also offers a lot of choice and variety as far as who your clients are, where you work, in what environment you will work, and how you can contribute to the development and lives of the parents for whom you work and their children.

Before you can plan the path to a successful career as a childcare professional, it's helpful to develop an understanding of what role you want to have and in what environment you wish to work. Do you want to work in an established organization, or do you prefer the more entrepreneurial feel of a private business? Do you want to work specifically with infants or children with special needs? Or maybe you want to travel and live the adventurous life of a nanny. Are you willing to relocate for your job? Work long hours and weekends? These are all things to consider.

Also important to think about: How much education would you like to pursue? Depending on your ultimate career goal, the steps to getting there differ. Jobs in childcare professions require a high school degree or equivalent in some but not all states. In many states, a childcare professional may need special training after high school in early childhood or child development in order to be qualified for employment.

Most employers will prefer working with a childcare professional who has at least a high school diploma and some training in early childhood. This training requirement is fulfilled through pursuing a college degree or earning credits in early childhood development. This chapter will discuss all these options, including explaining the differences between the different college degrees available in relevant fields that you may want to pursue.

Note: Requirements for education and certification fulfillments to be a childcare professional differ from state to state. Check the rules in your state to be sure you know what degrees or certifications you need to hold in order to work there legally.

Deciding on a career means asking yourself big questions, but there are several tools and assessment tests that can help you determine what your personal strengths and aptitudes are and which career fields and environments they best align with. These tools guide you to think about important factors in choosing a career path, such as how you respond to pressure and how effectively you work and communicate with people (as well as how much you enjoy it). These will be discussed in this chapter as well.

YOUR PASSIONS, ABILITIES, AND INTERESTS: IN JOB FORM!

Think about how you've done at school and how things have worked out at any temporary or part-time jobs you've had so far. What are you really good at, in your opinion? And what have other people told you you're good at? What are you not very good at right now, but you would like to become better at? What are you not very good at, and you're okay with not getting better at?

Now forget about work for a minute. In fact, forget about needing to ever have a job again. You won the lottery—congratulations. Now answer these questions: What are your three favorite ways of spending your time? For each one of those things, can you describe why you think you in particular are attracted to it? If you could get up tomorrow and do anything you wanted all day long, what would it be? These questions can be fun but can also lead you to your true passions. The next step is to find the job that sparks your passions.

This chapter explores the educational requirements for various careers within the childcare professional field, as well as options for where to go for help when planning your path to the career you want. It offers advice on how to begin preparing for your career path at any age or stage in your education, including in high school.

Planning the Plan

So where to begin? Before taking the leap and applying to or committing in your mind to a particular professional path, there are other considerations and steps you can take to map out your plan for pursuing your career. Preparing your career plan begins with developing a clear understanding of what your actual career goal is.

Planning your career path means asking yourself questions that will help shape a clearer picture of what your long-term career goals are and what steps to take in order to achieve them. When considering these questions, it's important to prioritize your answers; when listing your skills, for example, put them in order of strongest to weakest. When considering questions relating to how you want to balance your career with the rest of your nonwork life, such as family and hobbies, really think about what your top priorities are and in what order.

The following are questions that are helpful to think about deeply when planning your career path:

- Think about your interests outside of the work context. How do you like to spend your free time? What inspires you? What kind of people do you like to surround yourself with, and how do you best learn? What do you really love doing? (Hint: If you find you are impatient when others discuss their children, or dread events where children will be present, a future as a childcare professional may not be for you!)
- Brainstorm a list of jobs that fall under the childcare professional category or are closely related. This can include anything from pursuing a career as a physical education teacher to that of a researcher for a child development–focused charity. The point is to focus on what aspects of childcare appeal to you, and what jobs put a major emphasis on these.
- Research information on each job on your career choices list. You can find job descriptions, salary indications, career outlook, salary, and educational requirements information online, for example. Some of this information was provided in chapter 1 of this book.
- Consider your personality traits. This is very important to finding which jobs "fit" you and which almost certainly do not. How do you respond to stress and pressure? Do you consider yourself a strong communicator? Do you work well in teams or prefer to work independently? Do you consider yourself a creative thinker? How do you respond to criticism? Are you curious and thorough? All of these are important to keep in mind to ensure you choose a career path that makes you happy and in which you can thrive.
- Although a career choice is obviously a huge factor in your future, it's important to consider what other factors feature in your vision of your ideal life. Think about how your career will fit in with the rest of your life, including whether you want to live in a big city or small town, how

much flexibility you want in your schedule, how much autonomy you want in your work, and what your ultimate career goal is.

- The job of a childcare professional is one that can bring you up close and personal to the circumstances and challenges of another family's life—the good and the bad. Whenever your job involves helping people achieve balance in their lives—through providing a service that enables them to work and have a family, for example—you get insights into their lives that you may not have in other professions. You'll know whether a child was up all night having nightmares or has trouble focusing because they are excited about an upcoming holiday. You'll know about the good times and the more challenging ones. This comes with the wonderful feeling of connecting to others and the somewhat draining feeling of feeling too attached. It takes a lot of commitment to work with children, so be sure you are up for such demanding work—without burning out.

Although the job of a childcare professional can often be stressful and emotionally tiring if not difficult, it also comes with many rewards, including the bonds you form with children and their parents or primary caregivers, and the positive influence you are able to be.
sturti/E +/Getty Images

- Many job opportunities that offer experience to newcomers and recent graduates can come with relatively low salaries. What are your pay expectations, now and in the future?

Posing these questions to yourself and thinking about them deeply and answering them honestly will help make your career goals clearer and guide you in knowing which steps you will need to take to get there.

Where to Go for Help

Again, the process of deciding on and planning a career path can be a little bit daunting. In many ways, the range of choices of careers available today is a wonderful thing. It allows us to refine our career goals and customize them to our own lives and personalities. In other ways, though, too much choice can be extremely confusing and can require a lot of soul-searching to navigate clearly.

Note: Depending on your age and educational level, you might also be thinking you have time to consider these points more carefully. But the sooner you start thinking in terms of a particular career path, the better prepared you will be to spot opportunities that present themselves in your schooling or your life to advance your relative skill sets.

WHAT IS THE DIFFERENCE BETWEEN A PRESCHOOL TEACHER AND OTHER ELEMENTARY SCHOOL TEACHERS?

You may be questioning whether you want to teach early childhood education—preschool—or elementary-level education, usually kindergarten through sixth grade. These career paths are similar in many ways but different in other significant ones.

There are differences in level of education required, to start: typically, a preschool teacher must hold an associate degree, while an elementary school teacher must earn a bachelor's degree at minimum.

There are also differences in salary expectations. According to the Bureau of Labor Statistics, employment is expected to increase by 7 percent for preschool teaching between 2014 and 2024,[1] and 6 percent for elementary teaching in the same time frame.[2]

As far as skills needed, the following comparison is the result of research conducted by Rasmussen University in which seventy thousand job postings were analyzed and the following "ten most desired skills" identified.[3]

Desired skills for preschool teachers:

- Child development
- Childcare
- First aid
- Lesson planning
- Cleaning
- Music
- Psychology
- Record keeping
- Case management
- Scheduling

Desired skills for elementary school teachers:

- Lesson planning
- Mathematics
- Collaboration
- Staff development
- Scheduling
- Curriculum development
- Workshops
- First aid
- Community relations
- Decision-making

Answering questions about your habits, preferences, interests, and personality can be very hard to do—and to do honestly. Identifying and prioritizing all your ambitions, interests, and passions is tough. It's not always easy to see ourselves objectively or see a way to achieve what matters most to us. But there are several resources and approaches to help guide you in drawing conclusions about these important questions.

- Take a career assessment test to help you answer questions about what career best suits you. There are several available online, which you can find via your search engine.
- Consult with a career or personal coach to help you refine your understanding of your goals and how to pursue them.
- Talk with professionals working in the job you are considering and ask them what they enjoy about their work, what they find the most challenging, and what path they followed to get there.
- Educate yourself as much as possible about the field: What are the latest research breakthroughs or trends in child development, or in the particular "problem areas" you are interested in focusing on? What are the latest statistics about childcare or early education or other issues being faced by people in the United States and beyond? Stay current as much as possible with topics relating to the career you wish to pursue.
- See if there are any "job shadow" opportunities. Job shadowing means following a person around, more or less, during that individual's workday, observing what a typical day on the job entails. It's a great way to get a hands-on, realistic view at what it is like to perform a certain job for a living.

ONLINE RESOURCES TO HELP YOU PLAN YOUR PATH

The internet is an excellent source of advice and assessment tools that can help you find and figure out how to pursue your career path. Some of these tools focus on an individual's personality and aptitude; others can help you identify and improve your skills to prepare for your career.

In addition to these sites below, you can use the internet to find a career or life coach near you—many offer their services online as well. Job sites such as LinkedIn are a good place to search for people working in a profession you'd like to learn more about, or to explore the types of jobs available in childcare.

- At educations.com, you will find a career test designed to help you find the job of your dreams. Visit https://www.educations.com/career-test to take the test.
- The Princeton Review has created a career quiz that focuses on personal interests: https://www.princetonreview.com/quiz/career-quiz.
- There are career tests designed specifically for childcare professions and whether you are a fit for them. Here's an example, but you can find others online: https://selmar.edu.au/2018/01/quiz-work-child-care/.
- The Bureau of Labor Statistics provides information, including quizzes and videos, to help students up to grade 12 explore various career paths. The site also provides general information on career prospects and salaries. Visit BLS.gov to find these resources.

Note: Young adults with disabilities can face additional challenges when planning a career path. DO-IT (Disabilities, Opportunities, Internetworking, and Technology) is an organization dedicated to promoting career and education inclusion for everyone. Its website contains a wealth of information and tools to help all young people plan a career path, including self-assessment tests and career exploration questionnaires: https://www.washington.edu/doit/preparing-career-online-tutorial.

Making High School Count

Once you have narrowed down your interests and have a fairly solid idea what type of career you want to pursue, you naturally want to start putting your career path plan into motion as quickly as you can. If you are a high school student, you may feel there isn't much you can do toward achieving your career goals—other than, of course, earning good grades and graduating.

But there are actually many ways you can make your high school years count toward your career in childcare before you have earned your high school diploma. This section will cover how you can use this period of your education and life to better prepare you for your career goal and to ensure you keep your passion alive while improving your skill set.

Even while still in high school, there are many ways you can begin working toward your career goal. Classes in another language, in writing, in interpersonal communication, and in health can all help you prepare for a career as a childcare professional, as can working as a babysitter.
Courtney Hale/iStock/Getty Images

COURSES TO TAKE IN HIGH SCHOOL

Depending on your high school and what courses are offered and that you have access to, there are many subjects that will help you prepare for a career in childcare. Beyond gaining hands-on experience working with or looking after children, you can take advantage of any college prep courses your school offers, in areas relating to psychology or sociology, for example, but also in subjects such as communication or studying a second language.

CULTURALLY SENSITIVE CHILDCARE

A career as a childcare professional will bring the opportunity to work in various areas, be it a different country or city or area, in culturally diverse environments. A key practice for childcare is to provide culturally sensitive care—caring for children from culturally diverse families in ways that are consistent with their home practices and values.

When children are raised solely by their own family members, the fundamental identifying building block, culture, is passed along inherently. When other people outside of the family participate in the childcare, it's important to remain mindful of the child's culture, which is key to their confidence, competence, and connection as they grow and learn in the world.

Here are "five keys" to providing culturally sensitive childcare, as provided by the Virginia Head Start Association:

Provide cultural consistency

Childcare should be in harmony with what goes on at home. Young children need to feel good about where they come from. The child experiences similar patterns of care, senses the connection between childcare and home and, as a result, feels secure.

Work toward representative staffing

When the caregiver reflects the culture of the child, the parent and the caregiver are more likely to have a common vision of the person they want that child to become.

Create small groups

All infants benefit when they receive care in a small group. With small groups, caregivers have a manageable number of cultures to relate to. As a result, many misunderstandings can be averted.

Use the home language

Communication between a caregiver and a young child in the child's home language supports the child's identification with his or her family and culture. In addition to strengthening the connection between home and childcare, when caregivers use and understand the home language, an infant has an easier time getting his or her needs met.

Make environment relevant

The environment and materials of a childcare program should reflect the children and their cultures. By seeing pictures of themselves, their families, and their communities, children are given the message that who they are and where they come from is valued.[4]

Tip: Everybody harbors biases in the way they think about sensitive issues such as race and sexual identity. To find out whether you have biases you may be unaware of, check out this text online, which was developed at Harvard University: https://implicit.harvard.edu/implicit/takeatest.html.

Here are some courses, college prep or standard level, that you should pursue while in high school. Some of them may seem unrelated initially, but they will all help you prepare yourself and develop key skills.

- *Nutrition:* Childcare professionals are responsible for ensuring that children eat healthful and sensible diets under their care. A course in nutrition would be a great asset to anyone involved in food preparation or diet management.
- *Physical education:* A childcare provider is also tasked with making sure that children under their care are healthy as far as physical activity, so additional knowledge in this area will also be a big asset if you are coaching children, organizing gym activities, and helping them prevent or treat injuries.
- *Psychology/sociology:* These courses will help you understand how the human mind works, as well as how people interact, and give you a basic understanding of human behavior. All of this will be of interest to you if you want a future helping with the development and care of children.
- *First aid and cardiopulmonary resuscitation (CPR):* These are two very important certifications for childcare providers to have, as you may find yourself the first person to respond to life-threatening accidents such as near drownings or choking episodes. If such opportunities are not available through your school, check your local community for options.
- *Interpersonal communication/public speaking:* These courses will be an asset in any profession, but especially in childcare professions. You will be communicating with many other people when working with clients, as well as, of course, communicating with the children themselves; doing so effectively will be a major factor in your success.
- *A second language:* To expand your clientele and be able to reach more people in need of a childcare provider, learning a second language will be a great asset.

- *Business and economics:* If you imagine yourself running a private child-care business, you will need to have business and accounting skills.

Tip: Taking advanced placement (AP) courses while in high school (assuming you pass the AP exam at the end of the course) may enable you to earn college credit early and skip taking elementary or introductory courses in the subject (e.g., psychology) when you get to college.

GAINING WORK EXPERIENCE

The best way to learn anything is to do it. When it comes to preparing for a career as a childcare professional, you can consider volunteering in your community, school, or church, or babysitting, tutoring, or working at a day camp in the summer vacation months.

Volunteering or working paying jobs in this way will provide you valuable training in areas such as managing the emotional needs of children; flexing your creativity muscles as far as coming up with engaging activities for children; developing your own skills as a responsible, organized leader; and so on.

Find out if your school offers any opportunities for volunteering, such as a tutoring program or a reading group for young children in the public library. You can also contact community centers to find out about how you can help with fundraising initiatives or coaching youth sports teams or other activities. All these initiatives will help prepare you for a career as a childcare professional.

HOW CHILDCARE PROFESSIONALS PRACTICE "SELF-CARE"

This book has already touched on the fact that, despite childcare being a job that carries with it an undeniable "feel-good" factor if you love working with children, it also can be physically and emotionally draining. "Self-care" refers to the various ways people can ensure that they are looking after their own needs, eating and sleeping well, for example, or exercising to release energy and process thoughts in a healthy, beneficial way. Doing so can help anyone, but especially childcare professionals and others in similar care-focused professions, maintain their own sense of well-being so they are better prepared and able to help others and avoid burnout.

The following tips for how to practice self-care are provided by licensed social worker Jane E. Shersher.[5] These techniques also work for anyone in a physically and emotionally demanding job:

1. *Focus on your breathing:* Take long, slow, deep breaths as a way of maintaining your calm and relaxing your mind. Consider setting a timer to remind yourself to breathe in this way a few times a day for a minute or two at a time. It may sound a little strange to remind yourself to breathe, but doing so in this manner can lead to noticeable results.
2. *Do a body scan:* This might also sound a bit odd, but you can help your body and mind relax by paying attention to each body part one at a time from head to toe, concentrating on it and checking for points of tension to release.
3. *Guided imagery:* Visualize yourself in a place or an environment that helps to calm you down, inspire you, or aid you in focusing for stretches of time (a few minutes, for example). There are apps you can use to help you feel calm, such as apps that you can use to listen to soothing sounds, such as nature sounds.
4. *Practice mindfulness:* Mindfulness has certainly risen in popularity the last several years. It is the practice of focusing your awareness on the present moment, while noticing and accepting feelings, thoughts, and bodily sensations. There are several apps that offer guided mindfulness meditations that you can try.
5. *Practice yoga, tai chi, or qigong:* These are physical exercises for the body and mind, which help with mental focus, flexibility, and balance and can reduce anxiety. You can incorporate these several times a day.
6. *Get enough sleep:* Sleep is so important; it cannot be stressed enough. Your body should be getting, on average, seven to eight hours of sleep. Try to build a routine that helps you be able to fall into a sleepy state so you can have a restful night. Exercise, diet, and winding-down routines (like taking a bath, reading a book) can help.

Tip: Keep physical health in mind as well as mental. Consider practicing yoga to keep your limbs and muscles strong enough for the task of taking care of children for a living. If attending a class is difficulty with your schedule or wallet, there are many apps that can help you with getting started or keeping up with yoga or other forms of exercise.

Educational Requirements

As mentioned earlier, each state has its own requirements as far as educational level achieved to become a childcare professional in that state. In some cases, a high school degree is the minimal requirement. But in some positions within the childcare industry, such as if you want to pursue an administrative or supervisor role, additional training will be necessary. This can be in the form of a bachelor's degree or even a master's in early childhood or childcare education. This can also broaden your career track potential.

Whatever type of job you want to pursue in the childcare arena, you should expect to have to obtain national certification to gain employment, depending on the state. One such certification, for example, is the child development associate certification, which requires an applicant to hold a high school diploma and have some work experience. If you want to operate a childcare facility from your home, you will further need to obtain a license to do so, a process that entails paperwork and an inspection of the premises for approval.

HOW TO PREPARE FOR RUNNING
A CHILDCARE CENTER IN YOUR HOME

Although this chapter has already provided advice on the types of courses you should consider following in high school or higher education to help prepare you for success as a childcare professional, if you have the ambition to run your own private childcare business, you will gain from following even more business-related courses.

Running a business is its own challenge, on top of that of becoming a qualified childcare professional. Mastering certain business skills is absolutely crucial to succeeding in running your own childcare business, from doing your own accounting to getting the word out to attract clients. Here are some general tips for preparing to launch your own practice as a childcare provider:

1. *Accounting:* Take a basic accounting course. You will be responsible for managing the money for your business, and therefore, you will need to understand basic accounting concepts.
2. *Advertising:* Seek out courses that deal with the topic of advertising and promotion. Look into online classes that would be convenient and time efficient. Helpful topics are ones that deal with promotional design, cost-effective advertising techniques, and anything else that will help your business become prominent in the public eye.
3. *Social media marketing:* Today's professional doesn't just rely on word of mouth, business cards, and a nicely painted sign to increase the traffic flow of their business. Savvy business owners have mastered the world of Twitter, LinkedIn, Google+, Facebook, and so on. You may already have these skills under your belt, so begin to think in terms of how to effectively integrate them into the realm of a private childcare business. Begin to look at other childcare providers who are involved in marketing themselves through social media channels, and notice what you like and what changes you would make. Have fun with this—your imagination is your friend.
4. *Business plan:* Anyone planning on success has some concept of what it means to devise a business plan. Basically this is a well-researched, well-thought-out document that analyzes costs and projected income. This will be something you will need if you intend to seek out a loan from a bank and/or investor. If your college has a business major, go to the department offices and inquire as to the classes that might be appropriate for your endeavors. If this is not available or practical, begin to read online about what a business plan is and how to come up with one. Even if you do not plan on securing financial backing, a wise business owner always has a plan.
5. *Minor in business:* If you are convinced you will want to go into owning a private business, you might consider choosing business as your minor. It may sound like something you really do not want to do. However, if you go into private practice, it *will* be a fact that you *will* be doing business on a daily basis.

6. *Seminars on small business:* During your quarter or semester breaks, consider attending a small-business seminar. It will be a fast and easy way to get some basics under your belt; it will also give you a heads-up on what might lie ahead.

7. *Web design course:* Depending on finances, you may end up having to design a simple website for your childcare venture. But even if you plan on hiring someone else to do it, knowing what you're paying for is always smart business. Find out what attracts the eye and what doesn't. Discover what appeals to different age groups and target your clientele.

"The most challenging part of my job, I would say, is leaving the family. As time goes on, children grow, family dynamics change, and nannies do have to move on; this is the nature of the beast. Once you have formed an attachment to your charge and the family, it is extremely hard to say goodbye. It is like a period of mourning in a way, because you are saying goodbye to a part of your life and your heart." —Candi Vajana, newborn care specialist and nanny

WHY CHOOSE AN ASSOCIATE DEGREE?

You may be tempted to pursue an associate degree after earning your high school diploma. This degree takes comparably shorter time and course work to complete, as related to other advanced degrees you might consider, and if you are living near a community college, that adds a layer of convenience.

Note: In the world of childcare professions, a college degree is less of a requirement than are having the right certifications and qualifications and fulfilling state license requirements. Some will be mandatory to work where you live, and others will be optional but great to have to add to your résumé and attract the best jobs. There will be more on that in the next chapter!

A two-year degree—called an associate degree—is sufficient to give you a knowledge base to begin your career and can form as a basis should you decide to pursue a four-year degree later. You can earn, for example, an associate degree in childcare or in early childhood development. Programs will be discussed in more detail in the next chapter.

WHY CHOOSE A BACHELOR'S DEGREE?

A bachelor's degree usually takes four years to obtain. Although this level of degree might not be a requirement to get started with your career, in general, the higher education you pursue, the better your odds are to advance in your career, which means more opportunity and, often, more compensation.

The difference between an associate and a bachelor's degree is, of course, the amount of time each takes to complete. To earn a bachelor's degree, a candidate must complete forty college credits, compared with twenty for an associate. This translates to more courses completed and a deeper exploration of degree content, even though similar content is covered in both.

Note: Even when not required, continuing your education as far as possible can help advance your career, give you an edge over the competition in the field, and give you more specific knowledge relating to your work with child development or a related subject, such as nutrition or psychology.

WHY CHOOSE A MASTER'S DEGREE?

A master's degree is an advanced degree that usually takes two years to complete. A master's will offer you a chance to become more specialized and to build on the education and knowledge you gained while earning your bachelor's. A master's can be earned directly after your bachelor's, although many people choose to work for a while in between in order to discover what type of master's degree is most relevant to their careers and interests. Many people also earn their master's degree while working full- or part-time.

YOU HAVE TO HAVE A HEART FOR CHILDREN

Malou Kloet.
Courtesy of Malou Kloet

Malou Kloet is a Dutch pedagogical coach and owner of the Green House Kinderopvang, a day care center in the Netherlands that emphasizes caring for animals and nature. Kloet is an enthusiastic, socially focused childcare "all-rounder." Her drive to level up the pedagogical quality within Dutch childcare organizations arose when she started as a group leader at various childcare centers thirteen years ago. Her knowledge is rich, as she has extensive experience both "on the ground" caring for children and behind the scenes at management levels. In 2017, she graduated cum laude with a bachelor's degree in pedagogy.

Kloet specializes in writing pedagogical policy and its implementation. A go-getter and an improver, she encourages others through an active attitude to work. She is creative and enterprising, without losing sight of the (commercial) objectives, and a big fan of cross-fertilization and brainstorming sessions. Connecting professionals, parents, and children at different levels is her life motto. In her words, "Let's all look together at how we can make the educational offer for our (youngest) group of children as good as possible."

How did you choose childcare as a career?

As a very young child I always had a good connection with kids and especially younger kids. For example: when I attended a birthday, I always looked to see if there was a baby present somewhere. If so, I'd be sitting with the baby on my lap all the time, giving cuddles and a bottle, et cetera.

Can you describe your educational background and career path to date?

I completed vocational studies to be a pedagogical employee in 2008 and again in 2012. In 2013, I began my bachelor's program in pedagogy, and I graduated cum laude in 2017.

I followed a part-time work-study program for all three studies. This ensured that I could immediately apply what I learned in practice. I wasn't the type who wanted to sit in school five days per week.

Since 2008 I have been working as a teacher of kids between zero and four for small and big day care organizations. After I graduated with my bachelor's, I started in 2018 as an assistant manager in a location with four groups. Here I was allowed to supervise the location in setting up the location from A to Z: increasing parental involvement, setting up the educational program, and coaching the pedagogical staff. A great experience from which I learned a lot.

By coincidence, I started my own coaching agency in 2019. A small organization hired me to coach the pedagogical staff. Then the ball started rolling, and within a year I was working for six organizations as a freelance coach.

In 2020 I supervised a number of takeovers and inspection processes for locations that are under stricter supervision of the GGD, the Dutch health care service.

At the end of 2020 the location of Green House, my day care business, became available and I decided to take the step to a first small location. It was a very risky step, as it was the start of the coronavirus pandemic. Now, the day care is running well and I am in the planning stages of opening more small-scale locations under the same formula where playing outside and caring for animals and nature are central in the pedagogical vision.

What is a typical day on the job for you?

Typical in a day as a pedagogical teacher, business owner, and coach is that every day is different, chaotic, and beautiful at the same time. You never know what to expect, but wonderful moments always come.

What's the best or most satisfying part of your job?

I love seeing that a child is growing in her or his development, and that parents are happy if you guide them in the right way. I also love being there for parents as a listening ear without immediately judging or giving advice.

What's the most challenging part or stressful part of your job?

Keeping all the balls in the air is most challenging, both at home (my daughter is five) and at work. And all administrative work is not fun at all.

What has been the most surprising thing about your work in childcare?

That anyone in the Netherlands can open a day care center as a business, even people without a pedagogy-related degree (of course this is only possible if you have staff with a relevant degree).

What kinds of qualities and personal skills do you consider advantageous to doing your job successfully?

A work-learning trajectory is, in my opinion, in all ways the best education. You must have a heart for children. You have to be able to empathize, and you have to be able to work together. Creativity and good physical health arre also crucial. In addition, it is very important that the atmosphere in the team is good. If the atmosphere is not good, you will immediately notice that from the behavior of the children. It is therefore very important that you are social with your colleagues and that you can discuss matters openly with each other.

How do you combat burnout?

Good question. I think in any work (with children or adults) there can come a point where it's all too much. At that time, it's good to listen to yourself and learn to set boundaries with colleagues but maybe also with family and friends. So you can very well come out of a burnout stronger than ever. To prevent burnout, it is important to have a healthy lifestyle; healthy food, plenty of exercise, and enough sleep. *"Rust reinheid en regelmaat"* (rest, cleanliness, and regularity), we say in the Netherlands.

––––––––

Summary

This chapter covered a lot of ground in terms of how to break down the challenge of not only discovering whether a career as a childcare professional is right for you and in what environment, capacity, and work culture you want to work, but also how best to prepare yourself for achieving your career goal.

In this chapter, you learned about some of the specific training and educational options, requirements, and expectations that will put you, no matter what your current education level or age, at a strong advantage in your chosen field.

Use this chapter as a guideline for how to best discover what type of career will be the right fit for you, and consider what steps you can already be taking to get there. Some tips to leave you with:

- Take time to carefully consider what kind of work environment you see yourself working in. In the case of childcare professions, this obviously means you need to be sure that children being a main part of your environment is a crucial goal for you.

- Spend time with children, either babysitting, volunteering as a mentor (such as a Big Brother or Big Sister), tutoring smaller children, helping to coach a youth sports team, and so on, to see if you have an affinity for taking care of children.
- Talk with a working professional to get a feeling for what hours they keep, what challenges they face, and what the overall job entails. Find out what education or training they completed before launching their career, and what they really love about it or what challenges them.
- Think about how much time and money you want to invest in your education and training beyond high school. Investigate various colleges and certification options so you can better prepare yourself for the next step in your career path. (More of this in chapter 3.)
- Don't feel that you have to wait until you graduate from high school to begin taking steps to accomplish your career goals. Look for relevant classes you can take or ways in which you can start gaining experience.
- Keep work/life balance in mind. The career you choose will be one of many adult decisions you make, and ensuring that you keep all of your priorities—family, location, work schedule, salary—in mind will help you choose the right career for you, which will make you a happier person.

Chapter 3 will go into detail about the next steps–writing a resume and cover letter, interviewing well, follow-up communications, securing references, and more. This is information you can use to secure internships, volunteer positions, summer jobs, and so on. The sooner you can hone these skills, the better off you'll be in the professional world.

3

Pursuing the Educational Path

*M*aking decisions about your educational path can be just as complex a process as choosing a career in the first place. It is a decision that not only demands understanding what kind of education or training is required for the career you want, but also what kind of school or college you want to attend and, of course, how you are going to pay for it and balance it with the other commitments you have in your life, whether family or work. Everyone has different circumstances that need to be taken into consideration, be they geographical or economical. There is a lot to consider no matter what area of study you want to pursue, and depending on the type of job you want to have within the field of childcare.

Now that you've gotten an overview of the different degree options that can prepare you for your future career as a childcare professional, this chapter will dig more deeply into how to best choose the right type of educational and training plan for you. Even if you are years away from earning your high school diploma or equivalent, it's never too soon to start weighing your options, thinking about the application process, and of course taking time to really consider what kind of educational track and environment will suit you best.

Not everyone wants to take time to go to college or pursue additional academic-based training, and for many careers it is not required, even if recommended. And although a career in childcare is one you can, in some states, enter even without a high school diploma (check your state), it is always in your best interest to continue with your education as far as you can. Even if it takes longer because you are working while you complete your studies or earn childcare-related certifications (many of which are definitely required to work legally), the more you invest in your education and training, the further you can go in your career and the more you will earn.

So if you are interested in and prepared to follow the post–high school (or advanced) educational path, this chapter will help you navigate the process of deciding on the type of institution you would most thrive in, determining what type of degree you want to earn, and looking into costs and how to find help in meeting them.

The chapter will also give you advice on the application process, how to prepare for any entrance exams such as the SAT or ACT that you may need to take, and how to communicate your passion, ambition, and personal experience in a personal statement.

When you've completed this chapter, you should have a good sense of what kind of post–high school education is right for you and how to ensure you have the best chance of being accepted at the institution of your choice.

> **Note:** At the time of writing, the U.S. and beyond are recovering from a pandemic that has caused some of the traditional approaches to teaching and learning to change—hopefully just temporarily. This chapter is offering advice that assumes you will be applying to and attending educational institutions in person, which will hopefully be the case. Even if, for now, you are learning or doing "campus visits" virtually, the advice offered here is still relevant, even if the way you engage with institutions, faculty members, or other students is a bit unorthodox for the time being.

Finding a Program or School That Fits Your Personality

Before we get into the details of good schools that offer degrees in subjects related to childcare professions, it's a good idea for you to take some time to consider what "type" of learning institution will be best for you. Just as with your future work environment, understanding how you best learn, what type of atmosphere best fits your personality, and how and where you are most likely to succeed will play a major part in how happy you will be with your choice. This section will provide some thinking points to help you refine what kind of school or program is the best fit for you.[1]

CONSIDERING A GAP YEAR

Taking a year off between high school and college, often called a "gap year," is normal, perfectly acceptable, and even increasingly seen as a strong enhancement to a college application. Particularly if you want to pursue a career as a childcare professional, having exposure to the world outside of the classroom will help you gain perspective and experience that you can immediately apply to your future work. It can help you become more empathic, less judgmental, and a more open thinker. You can even use it as an opportunity to hone your skills (and discover more about how the profession suits you) in childcare, either by volunteering to teach English, working as a nanny, or finding another opportunity to work around children.

Because the cost of college has gone up dramatically, it literally pays for you to know going in what you want to study, and a gap year–well spent–can do lots to help you answer that question. It can also give you an opportunity to explore different places and people to help you find a deeper sense of what you'd like to study when your gap year has ended.

Some great ways to spend your gap year include joining the Peace Corps or other organizations that offer opportunities for work experience. A gap year can help you see things from a new perspective. Consider enrolling in a mountaineering program or other gap year–styled program, backpacking across Europe or other countries on the cheap (be safe and bring a friend), finding a volunteer organization that furthers a cause you believe in or that complements your career aspirations, joining a Road Scholar program (see www.roadscholar.org), teaching English in another country (see https://www.gooverseas.com/blog/best-countries-for-seniors-to-teach-english-abroad for more information), or working and earning money for college!

Many students will find that they get much more out of college when they have a year to mature and to experience the real world. The American Gap Year Association reports from its alumni surveys that students who take gap years show improved civic engagement, improved college graduation rates, and improved GPAs in college.

See the website at https://gapyearassociation.org/ for lots of advice and resources if you're considering a potentially life-altering experience.

If nothing else, answering questions like the following ones can help you narrow your search and focus on a smaller sampling of choices. Write your answers to these questions down somewhere where you can refer to them often, such as in your notes app on your phone:

- *Size*: Does the size of the school matter to you? Colleges and universities range from sizes of five hundred or fewer students to twenty-five thousand students. If you are considering college or university, think about what size of class you would like, and what the right instructor-to-student ratio is for you.
- *Community location:* Would you prefer to be in a rural area, a small town, a suburban area, or a large city? How important is the location of the school in the larger world to you? Is the flexibility of an online degree or certification program attractive to you, or do you prefer more on-site, hands-on instruction?

Note: You can also explore options with online courses for many childcare-related programs, including full bachelor's degree programs in child development as well as online courses in nanny training. Although there will likely be a requirement to complete some hours of supervised, in-person work directly with children to complete the program, a lot of coursework can be done online, adding flexibility and convenience and saving costs.

- *Length of study:* How many months or years do you want to put into your education before you start working professionally?
- *Housing options:* If applicable, what kind of housing would you prefer? Dorms, off-campus apartments, and private homes are all common options.
- *Student body:* How would you like the student body to "look"? Think about coed versus all-male and all-female settings, as well as the makeup of minorities, how many students are part-time versus full-time, and the percentage of commuter students.

- *Academic environment:* Consider which majors are offered and at which levels of degree. Research the student-to-faculty ratio. Are the classes taught often by actual professors or more often by the teaching assistants? Find out how many internships the school typically provides to students. Are independent study or study-abroad programs available in your area of interest?
- *Financial aid availability/cost:* Does the school provide ample opportunities for scholarships, grants, work-study programs, and the like? Does cost play a role in your options (for most people, it does)?
- *Support services:* Investigate the strength of the academic and career placement counseling services of the school.
- *Social activities and athletics:* Does the school offer clubs that you are interested in? Which sports are offered? Are scholarships available?
- *Specialized programs:* Does the school offer honors programs or programs for veterans or students with disabilities or special needs?

Note: Not all these questions are going to be important to you, and that's fine. Be sure to make note of aspects that don't matter so much to you too, such as size or location. You might change your mind as you go to visit colleges, but it's important to make note of where you are to begin with.

U.S. News & World Report puts it best when it says the college that fits you best is one that will do all these things:

- Offers a degree that matches your interests and needs
- Provides a style of instruction that matches the way you like to learn
- Provides a level of academic rigor to match your aptitude and preparation
- Offers a community that feels like home to you
- Values you for what you do well

MAKE THE MOST OF CAMPUS VISITS

If it's at all practical and feasible, you should visit the campuses of all the schools you're considering. To get a real feel for any college or university, you need to walk around the campus, spend some time in the common areas where students hang out, and sit in on a few classes. You can also sign up for campus tours, which are typically given by current students. This is another good way to see the campus and ask questions of someone who knows. Be sure to visit the specific school/building that covers your possible major as well. The website and brochures won't be able to convey that intangible feeling you'll get from a visit.

In addition to the questions listed earlier in this chapter, consider these questions as well. Make a list of questions that are important to you before you visit.

- What is the makeup of the current freshman class? Is the campus diverse?
- What is the meal plan like? What are the food options?
- Where do most of the students hang out between classes? (Be sure to visit this area.)
- How long does it take to walk from one end of the campus to the other?
- What types of transportation are available for students? Does campus security provide escorts to cars, dorms, etc. at night?

In order to be ready for your visit and make the most of it, consider these tips and words of advice. Before you go:

- Be sure to do some research. At the very least, spend some time on the college website. Make sure your questions aren't addressed adequately there first.
- Make a list of questions.
- Arrange to meet with a professor in your area of interest or to visit the specific school.
- Be prepared to answer questions about yourself and why you are interested in this school.
- Dress in neat, clean, and casual clothes. Avoid overly wrinkled clothing or anything with stains.
- Listen and take notes.
- Don't interrupt.

- Be positive and energetic.
- Make eye contact when someone speaks directly to you.
- Ask questions.
- Thank people for their time.

Finally, be sure to send thank-you notes or emails after the visit is over. Remind recipients when you visited the campus and thank them for their time.

Note: As mentioned earlier, given the current coronavirus pandemic and based on your personal choice of how you wish to pursue your communication, it is possible you will attend many of your courses online. However, many of the points will still apply, such as the student-to-professor ratio and the diversity of the student body.

The aim of this section has been to impress upon you the importance of finding the right fit for your chosen learning institution. Take some time to paint a mental picture about the kind of university or school setting that will best complement your needs. Then read on for specifics about each degree.

Note: In the academic world, accreditation matters and is something you should consider when choosing a school. Accreditation is basically a seal of approval that schools promote to let prospective students feel sure the institution will provide a quality education that is worth the investment and will help graduates reach their career goals. Future employers will want to see that the program you completed has such a seal of quality, so it's something to keep in mind when choosing a school.

Determining Your Education Plan

There are many options, as mentioned, when it comes to pursuing an education to prepare you for a career as a childcare professional. These include certification programs, two-year community colleges, four-year colleges, and master's programs.

HOW TO HAVE A GAP YEAR, EVEN IF YOU STAY HOME

Although an earlier section in this chapter explored options for spending a gap year that would certainly offer invaluable experience to an aspiring childcare professional, for many reasons, these options are not for everybody—but that does not mean there aren't enriching activities and pursuits you can engage in to make a gap year just as worthwhile.

NextAdvisor[2] offers some tips on how to make the most of a gap year, even if it is not possible to participate in a structured program such as the Peace Corps. While these tips may not seem as exciting as traveling abroad, the point of a gap year is to help you refine your interests and gain additional skills before committing yourself to a college program. Here are some options to consider:

- Learn a new skill. Learn a new language. Become an expert in building an online platform if you want to grow your own private practice or reach a broader audience in the future online. Take a photography course. It's a good time to really develop yourself in new areas that may directly or indirectly affect you as a social worker, in that it can help you to look at the world and people differently.
- Read. Science has shown that reading fiction makes us more empathetic,[3] which is a key skill for any social worker (or human, for that matter) to improve.
- Get a job to save money for college. Taking a year to earn money before heading off to school is certainly a valuable use of your time.
- Volunteer. There are virtual volunteer programs (check out VolunteerMatch), or you can do more local volunteering, such as for a children's organization or community center where children's activities are organized and held.
- Take online classes at a local community college in a related subject.

Whether you are opting for a two-year or four-year degree—and possibly later a master's—you will find there are many choices. It's a good idea to select roughly five to ten schools in a realistic location (for you) that offer the degree you want to earn. If you are considering online programs, include these in your list.

Tip: Consider attending a university in your resident state (where you live and pay taxes), if possible, which will save you lots of money if you attend a state school. Private institutions don't typically discount resident student tuition costs.

Be sure you research the basic GPA and SAT or ACT requirements of each school as well. Although some community colleges do not require standardized tests for the application process, others do.

Note: If you are planning to apply to a college or program that requires the ACT or SAT, advisors recommend that students take both the ACT and the SAT tests during their junior year of high school (spring at the latest). You can retake these tests and use your highest score, so be sure to leave time to retake early senior year if needed. You want your best score to be available to all the schools you're applying to by January of your senior year, which will also enable them to be considered with any scholarship applications. Keep in mind these are general timelines, so be sure to check the exact deadlines and calendars of the schools to which you're applying!

SAT IS OPTIONAL—SHOULD I TAKE IT ANYWAY?

One of the consequences of the coronavirus pandemic as it relates to education is that many universities changed aspects of their application processes. More than half of four-year colleges and universities in the United States—a staggering percentage—decided to make entrance exams like the SAT and ACT optional in 2021,[4] and this is a change that may persist for a lot longer.

What exactly does "test optional" mean? It varies from school to school. Be sure you know what it means for any school you are considering applying to:

- Truly test optional means you decide if you want to submit your test scores. If you do, the scores will be taken into consideration along with other parts of the application. This implies that the test scores may carry less weight when compared with the other application elements but will be considered.

- "Test flexible" schools will allow you to submit scores for the SAT or ACT, or a different test in their place (such as a SAT Subject Test or AP test).
- "Test blind" schools will not consider any scores, even if you include them in the application.

If you feel confident that your scores will be an asset to your application, then by all means take the test and submit the score. It will not hurt your chances and can only help them. And if you take the test and are not satisfied that the results will give your application a positive edge, then you are not obligated to submit the scores. So you really can't lose by preparing for and taking the tests.

Once you have found five to ten schools in a realistic location for you that offer the degree you want, spend some time on their websites studying the requirements for admissions. Important factors weighing on your decision of what schools to apply to should include whether you meet the requirements, your chances of getting in (but aim high!), tuition costs and availability of scholarships and grants, location, and the school's reputation and licensure/ graduation rates.

Note: Most colleges and universities will list the average stats for the last class accepted to the program, which will give you a sense of your chances of acceptance.

The order of these characteristics will depend on your grades and test scores, financial resources, work experience, and other personal factors. Taking everything into account, you should be able to narrow your list down to the institutes or schools that best match your educational or professional goals as well as your resources and other factors such as location and duration of study.

> **Tip:** References—recommendations from people with whom you've worked or studied—are a big part of an application either for a job or a training or degree program. For this reason, see every interaction you have as a professional or a student as an opportunity to build your application in the future. Never leave a bad impression so you cannot use someone later as a reference.

Schools to Consider When Pursuing a Career as a Childcare Professional

Some schools and programs have stronger reputations than others. Although you can certainly have a successful and satisfying career and experience without going to the "number one" school in your field of study, it is a good idea to shop around, to compare different schools and get a sense of what they offer and what features of each are the most important—or least—to you.

Keep in mind that what is "great" for one person may not be as great for someone else. What might be a perfect school for you might be too difficult, too expensive, or not rigorous enough for someone else. Keep in mind the advice of the previous sections when deciding what you really need in a school.

As mentioned previously, you have a choice of degree type you want to pursue in order to become qualified as a childcare professional. This section will point you to the best programs for associate, bachelor's, and master's degree programs.

GREAT SCHOOLS FOR EARLY CHILDHOOD EDUCATION: ASSOCIATE'S DEGREE PROGRAMS

The following lists the top online early childhood education associate degree programs as ranked in 2021—from number one to number ten—by Best Colleges.com.[5] Note this ranking lists online programs, which make earning your degree more convenient from wherever you live:

1. Southwest Wisconsin Technical College (based in Fennimore, WI)
2. Stanly Community College (based in Albemarle, NC)

3. Liberty University (based in Lynchburg, VA)
4. Northeast Community College (based in Norfolk, NE)
5. Vance-Granville Community College (based in Henderson, NC)
6. Community Care College (based in Tulsa, OK)
7. South Texas College (based in McAllen, TX)
8. Saint Francis University (based in Loretto, PA)
9. Kennebec Valley Community College (based in Fairfield, ME)
10. Randolph Community College (based in Asheboro, NC)

"It is not my job to raise them—they have parents and teachers for that. My job is to keep children in balance, to stimulate, motivate, and challenge them, and protect them, if necessary, in order for them to develop into self-sufficient young adults."
—Maria Ungurean, part-time nanny and student

GREAT SCHOOLS FOR EARLY CHILDHOOD DEVELOPMENT: BACHELOR'S DEGREE PROGRAMS

This list of the best schools offering undergraduate programs in early childhood development—from number one to number ten—has been compiled by CollegeChoice.net:[6]

1. University of Georgia (based in Athens, GA)
2. Arizona State University (based in Tempe, AZ)
3. New York University (based in New York, NY)
4. Florida Gulf Coast University (based in Fort Myers, FL)
5. Mercer University (based in Macon, GA)
6. Indiana University, Bloomington (based in Bloomington, IN)
7. University of Florida (based in Gainesville, FL)
8. Kennesaw State University (based in Kennesaw, GA)
9. University of Central Florida (based in Orlando, FL)
10. Georgia Gwinnett College (based in Lawrenceville, GA)

GREAT SCHOOLS FOR EARLY CHILDHOOD DEVELOPMENT: MASTER'S DEGREE PROGRAMS

This list of the best schools offering master's programs in early childhood development—from number one to number ten—has been compiled by CollegeChoice.net:[7]

1. University of Minnesota, Institute of Child Development (based in Minneapolis, MN)
2. SUNY at Albany (based in Albany, NY)
3. University of Alabama at Birmingham (based in Birmingham, AL)
4. Kennesaw State University, Bagwell College of Education (based in Kennesaw, GA)
5. University of Dayton (based in Dayton, OH)
6. University of La Verne (based in La Verne, CA)
7. Brenau University (based in Gainesville, GA)
8. Biola University (based in La Miranda, CA)
9. University of South Florida (based in Tampa, FL)
10. Northern Arizona University (based in Flagstaff, AZ)

THE REGULATORS OF CHILDCARE: LICENSING AND OTHER STANDARDS

The childcare profession is understandably a carefully regulated one. Understanding exactly which qualification you need to hold can be confusing and can vary state to state. Here is a rundown of childcare licensing regulations and other standards in the industry that may apply to your childcare business.

Licensing: A childcare license is verification that a childcare program meets the required standards for operating as such in terms of health and safety, sleep practices, caregiver-to-child ratios, size of group as a whole, food preparation and serving, training requirements for staff, sanitations, emergency preparedness (such as a fire escape plan), and thorough background checks for staff members. The standards are set by each state, and they do differ. Check with your local Child Care Resources and Referral (CCR&R) agency. Search for yours here: https://www.child careaware.org/resources/ccrr-search-form/. (Note: Not all childcare programs are required to have a license. To find out if a program is required to be licensed, contact your state licensing office.)

Accreditation: To really make your business stand out, you can become accredited by a national body that recognizes high levels of quality in childcare. Programs that wish to become accredited have to demonstrate they meet certain requirements above state licensing requirements. Contact your local CCR&R agency for more information on how to earn this accreditation in your state.

Quality rating and improvement system (QRIS): QRIS is mandatory in some states, but not in all. To find out more about this accreditation program, visit https://www.childcareaware.org/families/child-care-quality-ratings/.

What's It Going to Cost You?

So, the bottom line—what will your education end up costing you? First, some good news: According to *U.S. News and World Report*, the average tuition costs for colleges fell in 2020, which went against the standard trend of cost going up each year. For private colleges, costs fell by about 5 percent; for in-state colleges, the costs fell by 4 percent, and that of out-of-state (tuition for a person attending a state school but not in one's resident state) has fallen by 6 percent.[8]

Note: Also according to *U.S. News and World Report*, the cost of an out-of-state school compared with an in-state school is 72 percent higher,[9] so looking for a school in the state in which you are registered is definitely a way to cut down the costs of your education.

This trend appears to be continuing, according to an update by *U.S. News and World Report* that looks at tuition rates for the 2021–2022 school year.[10] This comes amid some calls for a tuition discount, as the COVID-19 pandemic has forced so many institutions to move to online course delivery.

In addition, there are several financial aid options to help you find the funding to earn the degree you want. We cover those next.

School can be an expensive investment, but there are many ways to seek help paying for your education.
marchmeena29/iStock/Getty Images

WRITING A GREAT PERSONAL STATEMENT FOR ADMISSION

The personal statement you include with your application to college is extremely important, especially when your GPA and SAT/ACT scores are on the border of what is typically accepted or if they are not a factor in your application at all. Write something that is thoughtful and conveys your understanding of the profession you are interested in, as well as your desire to practice in this field. Why are you uniquely qualified? Why are you a good fit for this university? These essays should be highly personal (the "personal" in personal statement). Pay particular focus to the aspects of working with children that appeal to you the most and why you feel you are particularly qualified and suitable to such a profession. Your communication style and personality will be major factors in your success in any role to do with childcare, so make sure both come through in your letter. Will the admissions professionals who read it, along with hundreds of others, come away with a snapshot of who you really are and what you are passionate about, and why?

Look online for some examples of good ones, which will give you a feel for what works. Be sure to check your specific school for length guidelines, format requirements, and any other guidelines they expect you to follow.

And of course, be sure to proofread it several times and ask a professional (such as your school writing center or your local library services) to proofread it as well.

Financial Aid: Finding Money for Education

Finding the money to attend college can seem out of reach. But you can do it if you have a plan before you actually start applying to college. If you get into your top-choice university, don't let the sticker cost turn you away. Financial aid can come from many different sources, and it's available to cover all different kinds of costs you'll encounter during your years in college, including tuition, fees, books, housing, and food.

The good news is that universities more often offer incentive or tuition discount aid to encourage students to attend. The market is often more competitive in the favor of the student, and colleges and universities are responding by offering more generous aid packages to a wider range of students than they used to. Here are some basic tips and pointers about the financial aid process:

- You apply for financial aid during your senior year of high school. You must fill out the FAFSA (Free Application for Federal Student Aid) form at studentaid.gov, which can be filed starting October 1 of your senior year until June of the year you graduate. Because the amount of available aid is limited, it's best to apply as soon as you possibly can. See fafsa.gov to get started.
- Be sure to compare and contrast deals you get at different schools. There is room to negotiate with universities. The first offer for aid may not be the best you'll get.
- Wait until you receive all offers from your top schools, and then use this information to negotiate with your top choice to see if the school will match or beat the best aid package you received.

- To be eligible to keep and maintain your financial aid package, you must meet certain grade/GPA requirements. Be sure you are very clear on these academic expectations and keep up with them.
- You must reapply for federal aid every year.

Note: Watch out for scholarship scams! You should never be asked to pay to submit the FAFSA form ("free" is in its name) or be required to pay a lot to find appropriate aid and scholarships. These are free services. If an organization promises you you'll get aid or that you have to "act now or miss out," these are both warning signs of a less reputable organization. Also, be careful with your personal information to avoid identity theft as well. Simple things like closing and exiting your browser after visiting sites where you entered personal information goes a long way. Don't share your student aid ID number with anyone either.

It's important to understand the different forms of financial aid that are available to you. That way, you'll know how to apply for different kinds and get the best financial aid package that fits your needs and strengths. The two main categories that financial aid falls under are gift aid, which don't have to be repaid, and self-help aid, which are either loans that must be repaid or work-study funds that are earned. The next sections cover the various types of financial aid that fit in one of these areas.

GRANTS

Grants typically are awarded to students who have financial needs, but they can also be used in the areas of athletics, academics, demographics, veteran support, and special talents. They do not have to be paid back. Grants can come from federal agencies, state agencies, specific universities, and private organizations. Most federal and state grants are based on financial need.

Examples of grants are the Pell Grant, SMART Grant, and the Federal Supplemental Educational Opportunity Grant (FSEOG). Visit the U.S. Department of Education's Federal Student Aid site for lots of current information about grants (see https://studentaid.ed.gov/types/grants-scholarships).

SCHOLARSHIPS

Scholarships are merit-based aid payments that do not have to be paid back. They are typically awarded based on academic excellence or some other special talent, such as music or art. Scholarships also fall under the areas of athletic based, minority based, aid for women, and so forth. These are typically not awarded by federal or state governments but instead come from the specific university you applied to as well as private and nonprofit organizations.

Be sure to reach out directly to the financial aid officers of the schools you want to attend. These people are great contacts that can lead you to many more sources of scholarships and financial aid. Visit http://www.gocollege.com/financial-aid/scholarships/types/ for lots more information about how scholarships in general work.

LOANS

Many types of loans are available especially to students to pay for their post-secondary education. However, the important thing to remember here is that loans must be paid back, with interest. Be sure you understand the interest rate you will be charged. This is the extra cost of borrowing the money and is usually a percentage of the amount you borrow. Is this fixed or will it change over time? Are the loan and interest deferred until you graduate (meaning you don't have to begin paying it off until after you graduate)? Is the loan subsidized (meaning the federal government pays the interest until you graduate)? These are all points you need to be clear about before you sign on the dotted line.

There are many types of loans offered to students, including need-based loans, non-need-based loans, state loans, and private loans. Two very reputable federal loans are the Perkins Loan and the Direct Stafford Loan. For more information about student loans, start at https://bigfuture.collegeboard.org/pay-for-college/loans/types-of-college-loans.

FEDERAL WORK-STUDY

The U.S. Federal Work-Study Program provides part-time jobs for undergraduate and graduate students with financial need so they can earn money to pay for educational expenses. The focus of such work is on community service work and work related to a student's course of study. Not all colleges and universities participate in this program, so be sure to check with the school financial aid office if this is something you are counting on. The sooner you apply, the more likely you will get the job you desire and be able to benefit from the program, as funds are limited. See https://studentaid.ed.gov/sa/types/work-study for more information about this opportunity.

THE POTENTIAL TO IMPACT MULTIPLE GENERATIONS

Joyce Ling.
Courtesy of Joyce Ling

After graduation from the College of Charleston, Joyce Ling began her career in education in 1982 when, as a young military spouse, she was hired to teach fifth grade at Fort Carson, Colorado. Since that time, while traveling the world with her spouse, she has taught at many different levels: fifth grade, fourth grade, preschool, and kindergarten. Joyce earned her master's degree from George Mason University with a master's in curriculum and instruction and literacy concentration. She currently serves as an ELA (English language arts) curriculum coach at an elementary school in Berkeley County, South Carolina. She has served in this role for the past six years.

How did you choose early child education as a career?

I like to say that I didn't choose my career in education but rather it chose me. While success in any career requires commitment and dedication, a career in education must be encompassed by a spiritual calling and a passion for the optimistic future of our country. The influence of a teacher has the potential to impact multiple generations. It is this impact that inspires me to continue my work in the field of education.

Can you describe your educational background and career path to date?

I grew up in Moncks Corner, South Carolina, a small town near Charleston. I attended public schools and graduated from the local high school. I chose to remain close to my hometown and attended and graduated from the College of Charleston with an MS in elementary education and a minor in English in 1981. I received a master's in curriculum and instruction with literacy concentration from George Mason University in 2003.

As a young military spouse, I began my career in education when I was hired to teach fifth grade at Fort Carson, Colorado. While at Fort Carson, we had our first child and then moved on to a new duty assignment. Several years later, our second child was born, and so as a young mother, I chose to stay home for a number of years to raise my children. In time, I reentered the education field when I was hired to teach Title I reading and then fourth grade in Fayetteville, North Carolina. Another military move brought me to teach fourth grade at Hampton Christian School in Hampton, Virginia. Later, while pursuing my master's degree in northern Virginia, I taught preschool part-time and also worked as a graduate research assistant at George Mason University. During our final year in northern Virginia, I served as the program liaison for the Advanced Studies in Teaching and Learning Graduate Program at George Mason University. Another military move took us to Fort Benning, Georgia, where I taught kindergarten for three years and then on to South Carolina where we have remained since. I taught kindergarten for an additional five years before assuming the role of the English language arts (ELA) instructional coach at my school. I have served in this position for the past six years.

What is a typical day on the job for you?

There really isn't a typical day for me as an instructional coach. Every day is different! One of the many roles of an instructional coach is to help teachers who may need extra guidance on their instructional practices. This may also include teachers who want to challenge themselves to learn new strategies. As a coach, I meet with these teachers to plan and implement research-based practices. I may provide observational feedback of their teaching, or I may coteach or model a lesson for these teachers.

Each week, I facilitate professional learning communities (PLCs) to collaborate and plan common instruction across grade levels. During these meetings, teachers plan along a scope and sequence and create lessons and common assessments. We also analyze data that teachers use to make revisions to instruction based on students' needs.

Another role of an instructional coach is to plan and conduct professional development at the school or district level. This requires research and planning to implement. Often, I collaborate with other instructional coaches to glean from their experience.

What's the best or most satisfying part of your job?

Hands down, the best part of my day is when I teach a lesson and have direct interaction with our students! When I leave school on those days, I feel fulfilled and content with my job. While my instruction may be in part to model a lesson for the classroom teacher, the satisfaction I receive by being in a classroom full of children is immeasurable.

What's the most challenging part or stressful part of your job?

Having just ended a school year during a pandemic, this is not an easy question to answer because there have been many challenges that arose during this most unusual school year. Even though this past year was unique, many of the challenges were not. As an instructional coach, I find that one of my biggest challenges is boosting morale for our teachers who are overwhelmed and exhausted from the demands of the job. Teacher burnout is real, and I do my best to inspire and encourage the teachers in my school, but I am not always sure my efforts are working.

What has been the most surprising thing about your work with early child education?

The most surprising thing I've encountered in all the years I've been in the education field is the change in families. When I began teaching, families were nearly all two-parent families. Parents were generally involved in their child's education, whether that meant serving as room parent, PTO member, classroom volunteer, or provider of supplies and snacks. The changes that have ensued as a result of single parenting, divorce, and/or grandparents raising their grandchildren (many of whom are working full-time as well) have cascaded into an evolution of nonengaged family members. I am saddened by the degradation of the family as we once knew it, but I am also encouraged by the resiliency of children who are our best hope for an optimistic future.

What kinds of qualities and personal skills do you consider advantageous to doing your job successfully?

Naturally, anyone in the field of education must first and foremost have unconditional and unending love for children. Anyone who believes they'll make it otherwise is sadly misguided. In addition, educators must consider themselves lifelong learners who are always looking for strategies that will engage their students and ensure their success. Sprinkle in lots of curiosity, patience, and tons of stamina, and there you have the qualities I believe are essential to success as an educator.

How do you combat burnout?

I believe it is critical that teachers consider their own social and emotional well-being a priority. Otherwise, they will never be able to pour into their students. My husband and I live on a small farm in the Low Country of South Carolina. It is there that I find my solace. The peace and quiet of country life afford me the opportunity to enjoy the beauty of nature and the companionship of our farm animals. Our farm is home to two horses, Buddy and Oreo; one barn cat, Leo; seven hens who provide us with farm fresh eggs; and our English bulldog, Winston.

═══════════════

Summary

This chapter covered all the aspects of college and postsecondary schooling that you'll want to consider as you move forward. Remember that finding the right fit is especially important, as it increases the chances that you'll stay in school and earn your degree as well as have an amazing experience while you're at it.

This chapter discussed how to evaluate and compare your options in order to get the best education for the best deal. You also learned a little about scholarships and financial aid, how the SAT and ACT tests work, if applicable, and how to write a unique personal statement that eloquently expresses your passions.

Use this chapter as a jumping-off point to dig deeper into your particular area of interest. Some tidbits of wisdom to leave you with:

- Take the SAT and ACT tests early in your junior year so you have time to take them again. Most universities automatically accept the highest scores, while some schools do not require these test scores at all.
- Make sure that the institution you plan to attend has an accredited program in your field of study. Some professions follow national accreditation policies, while others are state mandated and therefore differ across state lines. Do your research and understand the differences.
- Don't underestimate how important campus visits are, especially in the pursuit of finding the right academic fit. Come prepared to ask questions not addressed on the school website or in the literature.

- Your personal statement is a very important piece of your application that can set you apart from others. Take the time and energy needed to make it unique and compelling.
- Don't assume you can't afford a school based on the "sticker price." Many schools offer great scholarships and aid to qualified students. It doesn't hurt to apply. This advice especially applies to minorities, veterans, and students with disabilities.
- Don't lose sight of the fact that it's important to pursue a career that you enjoy, are good at, and are passionate about! You'll be a happier person if you do so.

At this point, your career goals and aspirations should be gelling. At the least, you should have a plan for finding out more information. Remember to do the research about the university, school, or degree program before you reach out and especially before you visit. Faculty and staff find students who ask challenging questions much more impressive than those who ask questions that can be answered by spending ten minutes on the school website.

Chapter 4 goes into detail about the next steps—writing a résumé and cover letter, interviewing well, follow-up communications, and more. This is information you can use to secure internships, volunteer positions, summer jobs, and more. It's not just for college grads. In fact, the sooner you can hone these communication skills, the better off you'll be in the professional world.

4

Writing Your Résumé and Interviewing

*W*ith each chapter of this book, the process of planning your childcare professional career path has narrowed, from the broadest of strokes—what childcare professionals actually do—to how to plan your strategy and educational approach to making your dream job a reality.

This chapter will cover the steps involved in applying for jobs or schools: how to prepare an effective, engaging, and informative résumé and slam-dunk an interview.

> **Note:** Whether you are applying for a job with an organization or to work directly for a family, how you present yourself in person and in writing will be a major determinant in your success and should receive just as much attention as the credentials you earn and the skills you hone.

Your résumé is your opportunity to summarize your experience, training, education, and goals and attract employers or school administrators. You can think of it like this: the goal of the résumé is to land the interview, and the goal of the interview is to land the job. Even if you do not have much working experience, you can still put together a résumé that expresses your interests and goals and the activities that illustrate your competence and interest.

As well as a résumé, you will be expected to write a cover letter that is basically your opportunity to reveal a little bit more about your passion, your motivation for a particular job or educational opportunity, and often to express more about you personally to give a potential employer a sense of who you are and what drives you. And particularly because you are striving for a career in a field that relies on interpersonal interaction and on personal characteristics as well as earned credentials, it's wise to ensure that your uniqueness, motivation, and commitment for working toward a meaningful cause—whatever your goal—comes through.

"Naturally, anyone in the field of education must first and foremost have unconditional and unending love for children. Anyone who believes they'll make it otherwise is sadly misguided. In addition, educators must consider themselves lifelong learners who are always looking for strategies that will engage their students and ensure their success."—Joyce Ling, early childhood educator

---

Giving the right impression is undoubtedly important, but don't let that make you nervous. In a résumé, cover letter, or interview, you want to put forward your best but your genuine self. Dress professionally, proofread carefully (spelling, grammar, and typographical errors will be noticed and will work against you!), but make sure you are being yourself.

In this chapter, we will cover all these important aspects of the job-hunting process, and by the end you will feel confident and ready to present yourself as a candidate for the job you really want.

Writing Your Résumé

Writing your first résumé can feel very challenging because you have likely not yet gained a lot of experience in a professional setting. But don't fret; employers understand that you are new to the workforce or to the particular career you are seeking.

Note: The right approach is never to exaggerate or invent experience or accomplishments, but to present yourself as someone with a good work ethic, a genuine interest in the particular job or organization, and use what you can to show yourself authentically and honestly.

There are some standard elements to an effective résumé that you should be sure to include. At the top should be your name, of course, as well as email address or other contact information. Always list your experience in chronological order, beginning with your current or most recent position—or whatever experience you want to share.

If you are a recent graduate with little work experience, you might want to begin with your education. If you've been in the working world for a while, you can opt to list your education or any certification you have at the end. List anywhere you have been published and any published work you may have edited.

Note: You may need to customize your résumé for different purposes to ensure that you are not filling it with information that does not directly link to your qualifications for a particular job.

SKILLS TO INCLUDE IN A CHILDCARE PROFESSIONAL RÉSUMÉ

The résumé is often a potential employer's first introduction to you, so it's important to present the most pertinent and relevant information about you in a brief, compact format. You want to let a person reviewing your résumé understand what you've done and what education you've completed, but also who you are and what you bring to your work as a childcare professional.

Here are some important skills you can include in a skills section, taken directly from and recommended by LiveCareer.com:[1]

1. Strong skills providing instruction to children
2. Excellent interpersonal and age-appropriate communication
3. Patience and self-control skills
4. High physical stamina and perseverance
5. Decision making, critical thinking, evaluation, and problem-solving
6. Ability to design, plan, implement, and lead educational programs and activities
7. Extensive knowledge of the needs of toddlers and infants
8. Provide emotional support for distressed children

9. Active listening and intentional communication
10. Ability to provide affection, security, and comfort
11. Building personal relationships with parents and children alike

If this is your first résumé, be sure you highlight your education where you can—any courses you've taken, be it in high school or through a community college or any other place that offers training related to your job target. Also highlight any hobbies or volunteer experience you have. But be concise; one page is usually appropriate, especially for your very first résumé.

Tip: Before preparing your résumé, try to connect with a hiring professional—a human resources person or hiring manager—in a similar position or organization you are interested in. They can give you advice on what employers look for and what information to highlight on your résumé, as well as what types of interview questions you can expect.

As important as your résumé's content is the way you design and format it. You can find several samples online of résumés that you can be inspired by. At TheBalanceCareers.com,[2] for example, you can find many templates and design ideas. You want your résumé to be attractive to the eye and formatted in a way that makes the key points easy to spot and digest; according to some research, employees take an average of six seconds to review a résumé, so you don't have a lot of time to get across your experience and value.

LINKING-IN WITH IMPACT

As well as your paper or electronic résumé, creating a LinkedIn profile is a good way to highlight your experience and promote yourself, as well as to network. Joining professional organizations or connecting with other people in your desired field are good ways to keep abreast of changes and trends and work opportunities.

The key elements of a LinkedIn profile are your photo, your headline, and your profile summary. These are the most revealing parts of the profile and the ones employers and connections will base their impression of you on.

The photo should be carefully chosen. Remember that LinkedIn is not Facebook or Instagram; it is not the place to share a photo of you acting too casually on vacation or at a party. According to Joshua Waldman, author of *Job Searching with Social Media for Dummies*,[3] the choice of photo should be taken seriously and be done right. His tips:

- Choose a photo in which you have a nice smile.
- Dress in professional clothing.
- Ensure that the background of the photo is pleasing to the eye. According to Waldman, some colors—like green and blue—convey a feeling of trust and stability.
- Remember it's not a mug shot. You can be creative with the angle of your photo rather than stare directly into the camera.
- Use your photo to convey some aspect of your personality.
- Focus on your face. Remember, visitors to your profile will see only a small thumbnail image, so be sure your face takes up most of it.

There are some standard elements to an effective résumé that you should be sure to include. At the top should be your name, of course, as well as email address or other contact information.

There is freedom and flexibility in how you organize the content of your résumé. The important thing is to present the most important and relevant information at the top. Your résumé needs to be easy to navigate and read.

WRITING AN OBJECTIVE

The objective section of your résumé is one of the most important, as it is the first section recruiters or hiring managers will read and therefore the first sense they will develop of you as a candidate. The objective should be brief but poignant. Definitely, it should be focused and give a sense of you as a unique applicant—you don't want it to be generic or bland—show how creative you can be while keeping it professional. It's important to take your time and really refine your objective so you can stand out and attract employers or clients.

Here are some sample objectives for a childcare professional résumé, taken directly from and recommended by LiveCareer.com:[4]

1. Seeking Child Care Provider position to contribute significant previous experience as camp counselor, professional babysitter, and part-time preschool assistant.
2. Responsible, dedicated Child Care Provider looking to utilize substantial childcare experience in maximizing educational and social experience for children at XYZ agency.
3. Experienced and committed college student with background in nutrition and child psychology seeking summer position as Child Care Provider at XYZ agency.
4. Looking for Child Care Position in dynamic and professional environment to contribute 10+ years of experience in caring for preschool and elementary school-aged children.

Be sure you do your research about the job and the organization you are applying to. Know exactly what kind of counselor the organization is looking for. Then you can better craft your objective to highlight the ways in which you uniquely match the position's needs.

Writing Your Cover Letter

As well as your résumé, most employers will ask that you submit a cover letter. This is a one-page letter in which you express your motivation, why you are interested in the organization or position, and what skills you possess that make you the right fit.

Here are some tips for writing an effective cover letter:

- As always, proofread your text carefully before submitting it.
- Be sure you have a letter that is focused on a specific job. Do not make it too general or one size fits all. Your personality and uniqueness should

come through, or the recruiter or hiring manager will move on to the next application.

- Summarize why you are right for the position. Keep it relevant and specific to what the particular individual or organization is looking for in a candidate and employee.
- Keep your letter to one page whenever possible.
- Introduce yourself in a way that makes the reader want to know more about you and encourages that individual to review your résumé.
- Be specific about the job you are applying for. Mention the title and be sure it is correct.
- Try to find the name of the person who will receive your letter rather than keeping it nonspecific ("to whom it may concern").
- Be sure you include your contact details.
- End with a "call to action"—a request for an interview, for example.

Interviewing Skills

With your sparkling résumé, LinkedIn profile, and writing samples, you are bound to be called for an interview. This is an important stage to reach: you will have already gone through several filters—a potential employer has gotten a quick scan of your experience and has reviewed your LinkedIn profile and has made the decision to learn more about you in person.

There's no way to know ahead of time exactly what to expect in an interview, but there are many ways to prepare yourself. You can start by learning more about the person who will be interviewing you. In the same way recruiters and employers can learn about you online, you can do the same (for a business or a professional in a business, of course—you should not be digging up information on a private family!). You can see if you have any education or work experience in common, or any contacts you both know. It's perfectly acceptable and even considered proactive in a positive way to research the person with whom you'll be interviewing, such as on LinkedIn.

Preparing yourself for the types of questions you will be asked to ensure you offer a thoughtful and meaningful response is vital to interview success. Particularly when you are applying for a job that will require and depend on how you present yourself conversationally and what kind of coolness under pressure you can maintain, it is paramount that you respond in an effective,

Be it in person or via video call, a job interview can be stressful. You can help calm your nerves and feel more confident if you prepare ahead by thinking about answers to questions you can anticipate being asked.
SDI Productions/E +/Getty Images

composed manner. Consider your answers carefully, and be prepared to support them with examples and anecdotes.

Here are some questions you should be prepared to be asked. It's a good idea to consider your answers carefully, without memorizing what you mean to say (as that can throw you off and will be obvious to the interviewee). Think carefully about your responses and be prepared to deliver them in a natural manner.

- Why did you decide to enter this field? What drives your passion for working in the childcare professional field?
- What is your educational background? What credentials did you earn?
- What experience do you have relating to working with children?
- Are you a team player? Describe your usual role in a team-centered work environment. Do you easily assume a leadership role?

BEWARE WHAT YOU SHARE ON SOCIAL MEDIA

Most of us engage in social media. Sites such as Facebook, Twitter, and Instagram provide us a platform for sharing photos and memories, opinions, and life events, and reveal everything from our political stance to our sense of humor. It's a great way to connect with people around the world, but once you post something, it's accessible to anyone—including potential employers—unless you take mindful precaution.

Your posts may be public, which means you may be making the wrong impression without realizing it. More and more, people are using search engines like Google to get a sense of potential employers, colleagues, or employees, and the impression you make online can have a strong impact on how you are perceived. Approximately 70 percent of employers search for information on candidates on social media sites.[5]

Glassdoor.com offers the following tips for how to avoid your social media activity from sabotaging your career success:[6]

1. Check your privacy settings. Ensure that your photos and posts are only accessible to the friends or contacts you want to see them. You want to come across as professional and reliable.
2. Rather than avoid social media while searching for a job, use it to your advantage. It's to your advantage to have an online presence (as long as it's a flattering one). Give future employees a sense of your professional interest by "liking" pages or joining groups of professional organizations related to your career goals.
3. Grammar counts. Be attentive to the quality of writing of all your posts and comments.
4. Be consistent. With each social media outlet, there is a different focus and tone of what you are communicating. LinkedIn is very professional while Facebook is far more social and relaxed. It's okay to take a different tone on various social media sites, but be sure you aren't blatantly contradicting yourself.
5. Choose your username carefully. Remember, social media may be the first impression anyone has of you in the professional realm.

Note: As a childcare professional, absolutely do not post photos on social media or share other content involving the children you are caring for in your work, unless you have explicit permission from a parent or guardian to do so.

Dressing Appropriately

How you dress for a job interview is very important to the impression you want to make. Remember that the interview, no matter what the actual environment in which you'd be working, is your chance to present your most professional self. Although you will not likely ever wear a suit to work—especially not if you are working with children!—for the interview it's the most professional choice.

Tip: A suit is no longer an absolute requirement in many job interviews, but avoid looking too casual as it will give the impression you are not that interested.

What Employers Expect

Hiring managers and human resource professionals will also have certain expectations of you at an interview. The main thing is preparation: it cannot be overstated that you should arrive to an interview appropriately dressed, on time, unhurried, and ready to answer—and ask—questions.

For any job interview, these are the main things employers will look for from you:

- You have a thorough understanding of the organization and the job for which you are applying.
- You are prepared to answer questions about yourself and your relevant experience.
- You are poised and likable but still professional. They will be looking for a sense of what it would be like to work with you on a daily basis and how your presence would fit in the culture of the business.

- You stay engaged. Listen carefully to what is being asked and offer thoughtful but concise answers. Don't blurt out answers you've memorized, but really focus on what is being asked.
- You're prepared to ask your own questions. It shows how much you understand the flow of an organization or workplace and how you will contribute to it. Some questions you can ask:
  - What created the need to fill this position? Is it a new position, or has someone left the organization?
  - Where does this position fit in the overall hierarchy of the organization?
  - What are the key skills required to succeed in this job?
  - What challenges might I expect to face within the first six months on the job?
  - How does this position relate to the achievement of the organization's (or department's, or boss's) goals?
  - How would you describe the organization's culture?

Note: When working with children, be sure to always inquire about particular preferences relating to diet, for example, or approach to managing difficult behaviors, with parents and supervisors.

You may find yourself interviewing virtually, using technology such as Zoom rather than appearing in person. This is almost certainly the case during the time of the pandemic, but it may also be your circumstance if you are applying to a job far away from where you live.

To prepare for an online interview, you should follow the same preparation tips as you would an in-person meeting, but be sure and test the technology ahead of time —including any application you need to use (e.g., passwords you require, microphone, camera). You can also test to see how your outfit or background appears to the person with whom you will be meeting. There is nothing worse than discovering your interviewee can't hear you properly or that there is anything unprofessional or inappropriate visible to the interviewee.

PROVIDING STRUCTURE THROUGH A LOVING NATURE

Maria Ungurean.
Courtesy of Maria Ungurean

Maria Ungurean, originally from Ukraine, moved to the Netherlands at the age of eighteen to study tourism and recreation management and international business management. To earn money while pursuing her studies, Ungurean began working as a part-time nanny. She says that the work has rewarded her and taught her in the greatest ways possible. "I have learned a lot about myself and, in a way, had a childhood do-over," she says.

How did you choose childcare as a career? Can you describe your educational background and career path to date?

I was studying international business management when I began working as a part-time nanny. Childcare is not related at all to my studies, but it has given me the flexibility for work that I needed. At first, picking up some babysitting hours was a great way to earn a living while staying on top of my schoolwork. Now, it has become more of a passion rather than a job. So, in short, I have no educational background in childcare, only practical experience gained by just doing it. For me, because I didn't have much of a childhood when growing up, in a way taking care of kids is my do-over at a childhood.

What is a typical day on the job for you?

Besides the obvious—preparing food, watching over the kids, and making sure that everything is going smoothly—a typical day would consist of at least one group activity. For example, while working with three kids of around one year apart, finding common interests is challenging but very efficient to making the day enjoyable for everyone. I believe that playing games, going for picnics, or even doing homework in a fun, playful way brings kids together and challenges them.

What's the best or most satisfying part of your job?

As I mentioned before, organizing activities to stimulate creativity and development is the most satisfying part of my job. The games children and I have come up with have been truly amazing. I once took care of a three-year-old child, for instance, who had not really learned how to communicate just yet, and she was immediately making up stories. It was incredible to see them thinking outside the box. Also, watching them grow and develop into young adults is truly rewarding! And of course, the most satisfying part of being a sitter is when the children express that they love you. It is something special.

What's the most challenging or stressful part of your job?

The most challenging part is to keep children in line and balanced while not ordering them around, if you know what I mean. I believe that it is most important that the kids are learning how to think for themselves as soon as it is genuinely possible. It is not my job to raise them—they have parents and teachers for that. My job is to keep children in balance, to stimulate, motivate, and challenge them, and protect them, if necessary, in order for them to develop into self-sufficient young adults. It is puzzling and on occasion stressful, but yet, so rewarding!

What has been the most surprising thing about your work in childcare?

While mostly concentrating on kids and their education, it is surprising how much you learn yourself in the process. I have learned how to crochet, knit, draw, and do many other things.

What kinds of qualities and personal skills do you consider advantageous to doing your job successfully?

In order for children to excel best, they need structure. In order to provide this for them firstly, they need to trust you. So being trustworthy would be first on my list. Patience would be second. Nobody needs a neurotic person screaming and shouting at them. It never helps and only causes trouble. Third, and most important, is a loving nature. Children need to know that you care for them as much as you want them to succeed.

How do you combat burnout?

Everyone has an off day sometimes, when nothing feels just right, and it seems that everything you touch fails. What helps in managing such days is to be honest about it. Children are very intuitive; they see when you are off. That's why I would always meet them with a big smile and ask them about their feelings and share mine, keeping it simple of course. You will be surprised how understanding they can be.

For example, one awful rainy day, the kids were exhausted of all the school-work and other activities. I hate pushing people, so instead the kids and I created a "lazy day." We all wore comfy clothes, watched movies, ate junk food, and just relaxed. What a crazy idea, many parents would think. However, the results were remarkable! For the rest of the week, none of the kids even wanted to look at the TV, which is a big thing for them, as you know. For the rest of the week, we only did activities, in- and outdoors. Everyone needs to hit the reset button sometimes, and in my case I do it with the children. That's the way I do it, and it keeps both myself and the children from burning out.

Summary

Congratulations on working through the book! You should now have a strong idea of your career goals within the childcare field and how to realize them. This chapter covered how to present yourself as the right candidate to a potential employer—and these strategies are also relevant if you are applying to a college or another form of training.

Here are some tips to sum it up:

- Your résumé should be concise and focused on only relevant aspects of your work experience or education. Although you can include some personal hobbies or details, they should be related to the job and your qualifications for it.
- Take your time with all your professional documents—your résumé, your cover letter, your LinkedIn profile—and be sure to proofread very carefully to avoid embarrassing and sloppy mistakes.
- Prepare yourself for an interview by anticipating the types of questions you will be asked and coming up with professional and meaningful responses.
- Equally, prepare some questions for your potential employer to ask at the interview. This will show you have a good understanding and interest in the organization and what role you would have in it.
- Always follow up after an interview with a letter or an email. An email is the fastest way to express your gratitude for the interviewer's time and restate your interest in the position.

- Dress appropriately for an interview, and pay extra attention to tidiness and hygiene.
- Be wary of what you share on social media sites while job searching. Most employers research candidates online, and what you have shared will influence their idea of who you are and what it would be like to work with you.

You've chosen to pursue a career in a competitive, challenging, but also broad and exciting field. I wish you great success in your future.

Notes

Introduction

1. U.S. Bureau of Labor Statistics, "Childcare Workers," accessed May 28, 2021, https://www.bls.gov/ooh/personal-care-and-service/childcare-workers.htm.

Chapter 1

1. Annamarya Scaccia, "How to Be a Good Babysitter: 11 Tips," Healthline, July 12, 2016, accessed June 2, 2021, https://www.healthline.com/health/parenting/how -to-be-a-good-babysitter.

2. Jo Adetunji, "To Fix America's Child Care, Let's Look at the Past," The Conversation, August 31, 2016, accessed June 2, 2021, https://theconversation.com/to-fix -americas-child-care-lets-look-at-the-past-63913.

3. Early Childhood History, "Historical Foundations of Early Childhood Education," accessed June 2, 2021, https://earlychildhoodhistory.weebly.com/origins-of -childcare-in-the-united-states.html.

4. RaiseMe.com, "Childcare Workers: Salary, Career Path, Job Outlook, Education and More," accessed June 2, 2021, https://www.raise.me/careers/personal -care-and-service/childcare-workers.

5. U.S. Bureau of Labor Statistics, "Childcare Workers," accessed May 28, 2021, https://www.bls.gov/ooh/personal-care-and-service/childcare-workers.htm.

6. Jill Cedar, "Childcare Costs," VeryWellFamily.com, June 22, 2020, accessed June 2, 2021, https://www.verywellfamily.com/affording-child-care-4157342.

Chapter 2

1. U.S. Bureau of Labor Statistics, "Preschool Teachers," accessed June 3, 2021, https://www.bls.gov/ooh/education-training-and-library/preschool-teachers .htm#tab-6.

2. U.S. Bureau of Labor Statistics, "Kindergarten and Elementary School Teachers," accessed June 3, 2021, https://www.bls.gov/ooh/Education-Training-and-Library/Kindergarten-and-elementary-school-teachers.htm#tab-6.

3. Brianna Flavin, "Early Childhood Education vs. Elementary Education: Which Environment Is Right for You?" Rasmussen University, May 23, 2015, accessed June 3, 2021, https://www.rasmussen.edu/degrees/education/blog/early-childhood-education-vs-elementary-education/.

4. Virginia Head Start Association, "First Five Keys to Culturally Sensitive Child Care," accessed June 3, 2021, https://www.headstartva.org/assets/docs/First-Five-Keys-to-Culturally-Sensitive-Child-Care.pdf.

5. Jane E. Shersher, "Self Care Tips for Social Workers," SocialWorkLicensure.org, accessed April 21, 2021, https://socialworklicensure.org/articles/self-care-tips/.

Chapter 3

1. Steven R. Antonoff, "College Personality Quiz," *U.S. News and World Report*, July 31, 2018, accessed May 21, 2021, https://www.usnews.com/education/best-colleges/right-school/choices/articles/college-personality-quiz.

2. Alex Gailey, "Taking a Gap Year during Coronavirus? Here's How to Make the Most of It," NextAdvisor, September 29, 2020, accessed May 21, 2021, https://time.com/nextadvisor/in-the-news/gap-year-coronavirus/.

3. Claudia Hammond, "Does Reading Fiction Make Us Better People?" BBC.com, June 3, 2019, accessed March 2, 2021, https://www.bbc.com/future/article/20190523-does-reading-fiction-make-us-better-people.

4. FairTest, "1,425+ Accredited, 4-Year Colleges & Universities with ACT/SAT-Optional Testing Policies for Fall, 2022 Admissions," last updated May 17, 2021, accessed May 21, 2021, https://fairtest.org/university/optional.

5. BestColleges.com, "Best Online Associate in Early Childhood Education Programs," accessed June 15, 2021, https://www.bestcolleges.com/features/top-online-associate-early-childhood-education-programs/.

6. CollegeChoice.net, "Top 10 Best Early Childhood Education Degrees," April 8, 2021, accessed June 14, 2021, https://www.collegechoice.net/rankings/best-early-childhood-education-degrees/.

7. CollegeChoice.net, "Best Master's in Child Development Degrees," May 28, 2021, accessed June 14, 2021, https://www.collegechoice.net/rankings/best-masters-in-child-development-degrees/.

8. Farran Powell and Emma Kerr, "See the Average College Tuition in 2020–2021," *U.S. News and World Report*, September 14, 2020, accessed May 2, 2021, https://www.usnews.com/education/best-colleges/paying-for-college/articles/paying-for-college-infographic.

9. Powell and Kerr, "See the Average College Tuition in 2020–2021."

10. Emma Kerr, "How Colleges Are Adjusting Their 2021–2022 Tuition." *U.S. News and World Report*, January 21, 2021, accessed May 2, 2021, https://www.usnews.com/education/best-colleges/paying-for-college/articles/how-colleges-are-adjusting-their-2021-2022-tuition.

Chapter 4

1. LiveCareer.com, "Child Care Provider Resume Objective Example," accessed June 17, 2021. https://www.livecareer.com/resume/objectives/child-care/provider.

2. The Balance Careers, "Student Resume Examples, Templates, and Writing Tips," accessed May 21, 2021, https://www.thebalancecareers.com/student-resume-examples-and-templates-2063555.

3. Joshua Waldman, *Job Searching with Social Media for Dummies* (Hoboken, NJ: Wiley and Sons, 2013).

4. LiveCareer.com, "Child Care Provider Resume Objective Example."

5. SecurityMagazine.com, "70 Percent of Employers Check Candidates' Social Media Profiles," September 23, 2018, accessed May 21, 2021, https://www.securitymagazine.com/gdpr-policy?url=https%3A%2F%2Fwww.securitymagazine.com%2Farticles%2F89441-percent-of-employers-check-candidates-social-media-profiles.

6. Alice A. M. Underwood, "9 Things to Avoid on Social Media While Looking for a New Job," Glassdoor, January 3, 2018, accessed October 30, 2020, https://www.glassdoor.com/blog/things-to-avoid-on-social-media-job-search/.

Glossary

Au pair: A young person, usually from another country or speaking another language from the family for which they work, who cares for children and does domestic work for a family in return for room and board and the opportunity to learn the family's language.

Babysitting: A general term for caring for children—including but not only babies—while parents or primary caregivers are unable to, such as during working hours or going out socially at night.

Bachelor's degree: A four-year degree awarded by a college or university.

Burnout: Feeling of physical and emotional exhaustion caused by overworking.

Campus: The location of a school, college, or university.

Career assessment test: A test that asks questions particularly geared to identify skills and interests to help inform the test taker on what type of career would suit them.

Childcare: A service that provides caring for children while parents or primary caregivers cannot, such as while they are at work. Childcare is usually provided in a private home, in a nursery or day care center, or at a preschool.

Child development: The process by which a child changes over time, including physical growth, intellectual growth, and language, emotional, and social development.

Colleagues: The people with which you work.

Community college: A two-year college that awards associate degrees.

Cover letter: A document that usually accompanies a résumé and allows candidates applying to a job or a school or internship an opportunity to describe their motivation and qualifications.

Day care: Day care centers, also sometimes called nursery schools, are businesses that provides supervision and care of infants and young children during the daytime.

Educational background: The degrees a person has earned and schools attended.

Empathy: The quality of being able to understand the feelings of another person.

Entry level: A position in a career usually held by individuals just starting out in their professional life, with their first professional job. Usually this indicates a lower salary and level of responsibility to start than jobs held by more experienced workers.

Financial aid: Various means of receiving financial support for the purposes of attending school. This can be a grant or scholarship, for example.

Gap year: A year between high school and higher education or employment during which individuals can explore their passions and interests, often while traveling.

General Education Development (GED) degree: A degree earned that is the equivalent to a high school diploma without graduating from high school.

Industry: The people and activities involved in one type of business, such as the business of childcare.

In-state school: A nonprivate college that exists in the state in which you are a resident. In-state schools offer lower tuitions to state residents.

Internship: A work experience opportunity that lasts for a set period of time and can be paid or unpaid.

Interpersonal skills: The ability to communicate and interact with other people in an effective manner.

Interviewing: A part of the job-seeking process in which candidates meet with a potential employer, usually face-to-face, in order to discuss their work experience and education and seek information about the position.

Job market: A market in which employers search for employees and employees search for jobs.

Kindergarten: A program or class for four-year-old to six-year-old children that serves as an introduction to school. Kindergarten is mandatory in some but not all states.

Major: The subject or course of study in which you choose to earn your degree.

Master's degree: A degree that is sought by those who have already earned a bachelor's degree in order to further their education.

Mental health: A person's health regarding their psychological and emotional well-being.

Mindfulness: The practice of focusing awareness on the present moment, while calmly acknowledging and accepting one's feelings, thoughts, and bodily sensations, used as a therapeutic technique.

Music and art therapy: Therapy in which music and art are used to help clients experience, articulate, and engage with emotions.

Networking: The processes of building, strengthening, and maintaining professional relationships as a way to further your career goals.

Nonjudgmental behavior: The ability to observe and accept another without qualifying a behavior as "right" or "wrong."

Nurture: To care for and protect (someone or something) while they are growing.

Out-of-state school: A nonprivate college that exists in a state other than in which you are a resident. These schools have higher tuitions for out-of-state residents.

Preschool: Also known as nursery school or play school, preschool is an educational learning space offered to children before they begin attending compulsory elementary school.

Private practice: An independent business—including that of a childcare provider—that is not controlled or paid for by the government or a larger company.

Psychology: The scientific study of the human mind and its functions.

Résumé: A document, usually one page, that outlines a person's professional experience and education, which is designed to give potential employers a sense of a candidate's qualifications.

Self-esteem: A term for confidence in one's own worth or abilities; self-respect.

Social media: Websites and applications that enable users to create and share content online for networking and social-sharing purposes. Examples include Facebook and Instagram.

Sociology: The study of the development, structure, and functioning of human society.

Special education teacher: A person who educates children who face physical, mental, emotional, and learning disabilities.

Tuition: The money you have to pay for education, be it a university degree or a certification.

Work culture: A concept that defines the beliefs, philosophy, thought processes, and attitudes of employees in a particular organization.

Yoga: A type of exercise in which you move your body into various positions in order to become more fit or flexible, to improve your breathing, and to relax your mind.

Further Resources

The following organizations, publications, and websites can help you further investigate and educate yourself on childcare-related topics, all of which will help you as you take the next steps in your career, now and throughout your professional life.

Organizations

NATIONAL ASSOCIATION FOR THE EDUCATION OF YOUNG CHILDREN

https://www.naeyc.org/
An organization committed to ensuring that the early childhood profession exemplifies excellence and is recognized as performing a vital role in society.

CHILDHOOD EDUCATION INTERNATIONAL

https://ceinternational1892.org/
An international organization working to develop and amplify innovative solutions to significant education challenges worldwide.

NATIONAL HEAD START ORGANIZATION

https://www.nhsa.org/
A nonprofit organization committed to the belief that every child, regardless of circumstances at birth, has the ability to succeed in life.

COUNCIL FOR EXCEPTIONAL CHILDREN

https://exceptionalchildren.org/
An international professional organization dedicated to improving the success of children and youth with disabilities and/or gifts and talents.

NATIONAL ASSOCIATION FOR FAMILY CHILD CARE

https://nafcc.org/

A nationwide nonprofit organization dedicated to promoting high-quality childcare by strengthening the profession of family childcare.

Publications

NANNY MAGAZINE

https://nannymag.com/

The premier trade magazine for the in-home childcare industry offering information and advice to professional nannies.

EXCHANGE MAGAZINE

https://www.childcareexchange.com/

Provides childcare professionals with practical ideas and proven strategies for dealing with the day-to-day challenges of administering an early childhood program.

Bibliography

Adetunji, Jo. "To Fix America's Child Care, Let's Look at the Past." The Conversation. August 31, 2016. Accessed June 2, 2021. https://theconversation.com/to-fix-americas-child-care-lets-look-at-the-past-63913.

Antonoff, Steven R. "College Personality Quiz." *U.S. News and World Report*, July 31, 2018. Accessed May 21, 2021. https://www.usnews.com/education/best-colleges/right-school/choices/articles/college-personality-quiz.

The Balance Careers. "Student Resume Examples, Templates, and Writing Tips." Accessed May 21, 2021. https://www.thebalancecareers.com/student-resume-examples-and-templates-2063555.

BestColleges.com. "Best Online Associate in Early Childhood Education Programs." Accessed June 15, 2021. https://www.bestcolleges.com/features/top-online-associate-early-childhood-education-programs/.

Cedar, Jill. "Childcare Costs." VeryWellFamily.com. June 22, 2020. Accessed June 2, 2021. https://www.verywellfamily.com/affording-child-care-4157342.

CollegeChoice.net. "Best Master's in Child Development Degrees." May 28, 2021. Accessed June 14, 2021. https://www.collegechoice.net/rankings/best-masters-in-child-development-degrees/.

———. "Top 10 Best Early Childhood Education Degrees." April 8, 2021. Accessed June 14, 2021. https://www.collegechoice.net/rankings/best-early-childhood-education-degrees/.

Early Childhood History. "Historical Foundations of Early Childhood Education." Accessed June 2, 2021. https://earlychildhoodhistory.weebly.com/origins-of-childcare-in-the-united-states.html.

FairTest. "1,425+ Accredited, 4-Year Colleges & Universities with ACT/SAT-Optional Testing Policies for Fall, 2022 Admissions." Last updated May 17, 2021. Accessed May 21, 2021. https://fairtest.org/university/optional.

Flavin, Brianna. "Early Childhood Education vs. Elementary Education: Which Environment Is Right for You?" Rasmussen University. May 23,

2015. Accessed June 3, 2021. https://www.rasmussen.edu/degrees/educa
tion/blog/early-childhood-education-vs-elementary-education/.

Gailey, Alex. "Taking a Gap Year during Coronavirus? Here's How to Make the
Most of It." NextAdvisor. September 29, 2020. Accessed May 21, 2021.
https://time.com/nextadvisor/in-the-news/gap-year-coronavirus/.

Hammond, Claudia. "Does Reading Fiction Make Us Better People?" BBC.
com. June 3, 2019. Accessed March 2, 2021. https://www.bbc.com/future/
article/20190523-does-reading-fiction-make-us-better-people.

Kerr, Emma. "How Colleges Are Adjusting Their 2021–2022 Tuition." *U.S.
News and World Report*, January 21, 2021. Accessed May 2, 2021. https://
www.usnews.com/education/best-colleges/paying-for-college/articles/
how-colleges-are-adjusting-their-2021-2022-tuition.

LiveCareer.com. "Child Care Provider Resume Objective Example." Accessed
June 17, 2021. https://www.livecareer.com/resume/objectives/child-care/
provider.

Powell, Farran, and Emma Kerr. "See the Average College Tuition in 2020–
2021." *U.S. News and World Report*, September 14, 2020. Accessed May
2, 2021. https://www.usnews.com/education/best-colleges/paying-for-col
lege/articles/paying-for-college-infographic.

RaiseMe.com. "Childcare Workers: Salary, Career Path, Job Outlook, Education and More." Accessed June 2, 2021. https://www.raise.me/careers/
personal-care-and-service/childcare-workers.

Scaccia, Annamarya. "How to Be a Good Babysitter: 11 Tips." Healthline. July
12, 2016. Accessed June 2, 2021. https://www.healthline.com/health/par
enting/how-to-be-a-good-babysitter.

SecurityMagazine.com. "70 Percent of Employers Check Candidates' Social
Media Profiles." September 23, 2018. Accessed May 21, 2021. https://
www.securitymagazine.com/gdpr-policy?url=https%3A%2F%2Fwww
.securitymagazine.com%2Farticles%2F89441-percent-of-employers
-check-candidates-social-media-profiles.

Shersher, Jane E. "Self Care Tips for Social Workers." SocialWorkLicensure.
org. Accessed April 21, 2021. https://socialworklicensure.org/articles/self
-care-tips/.

Underwood, Alice A.M. "9 Things to Avoid on Social Media While Looking
for a New Job." Glassdoor. January 3, 2018. Accessed October 30, 2020.

https://www.glassdoor.com/blog/things-to-avoid-on-social-media-job
-search/.

U.S. Bureau of Labor Statistics. "Childcare Workers." Accessed May 28, 2021.
https://www.bls.gov/ooh/personal-care-and-service/childcare-workers
.htm.

———. "Kindergarten and Elementary School Teachers." Accessed June 3,
2021. https://www.bls.gov/ooh/Education-Training-and-Library/Kinder
garten-and-elementary-school-teachers.htm#tab-6.

———. "Preschool Teachers." Accessed June 3, 2021. https://www.bls.gov/ooh/
education-training-and-library/preschool-teachers.htm#tab-6.

Virginia Head Start Association. "First Five Keys to Culturally Sensitive Child
Care." Accessed June 3, 2021. https://www.headstartva.org/assets/docs/
First-Five-Keys-to-Culturally-Sensitive-Child-Care.pdf.

Waldman, Joshua. *Job Searching with Social Media for Dummies.* Hoboken, NJ:
Wiley and Sons, 2013.

About the Author

Tracy Brown Hamilton is a writer, editor, and journalist based in the Netherlands. She has written several books on topics ranging from careers to media, economics to pop culture. She lives with her husband and three children.

Lightning Source UK Ltd.
Milton Keynes UK
UKHW011406140622
404419UK00011B/87

9 781538 159262